W9-ASE-149

Poetry and Wisdom

Regis College Library
15 ST. MARY STREET
TORONTO, ONTARIO, CANADA
M4Y 2R5

Tremper Longman III
General Editor and Old Testament Editor

Craig A. Evans
New Testament Editor

 BIBLIOGRAPHIES No. 3

Poetry and Wisdom

Peter Enns

BS
1405
.2
E55
1997

Regis College Library
15 ST. MARY STREET
TORONTO, ONTARIO, CANADA
M4Y 2R5

Baker Books
A Division of Baker Book House Co
Grand Rapids, Michigan 49516

© 1997 by The Institute for Biblical Research

Published by Baker Books
a division of Baker Book House Company
P.O. Box 6287, Grand Rapids, MI 49516-6287

Printed in the United States of America

All rights reserved. No part of this publication may be reproduced, stored in a retrieval system, or transmitted in any form or by any means—for example, electronic, photocopy, recording—without the prior written permission of the publisher. The only exception is brief quotations in printed reviews.

Library of Congress Cataloging-in-Publication Data

Enns, Peter, 1961–
    Poetry and wisdom / Peter Enns.
    p. cm. — (IBR bibliographies ; no. 3)
    Includes bibliographical references and index.
    ISBN 0-8010-2161-8 (pbk.)
    1. Hebrew poetry, Biblical—History and criticism—Bibliography.
    2. Wisdom literature—Criticism, interpretation, etc.—Bibliography.
    I. Title. II. Series.
    Z7772.B6E55   1998
    [BS1405.2]
    016.2216′6—dc21   97-33543

For information about academic books, resources for Christian leaders, and all new releases available from Baker Book House, visit our web site:
http://www.bakerbooks.com

Contents

Series Preface

With the proliferation of journals and publishing houses dedicated to biblical studies, it has become impossible for even the most dedicated scholar to keep in touch with the vast materials now available for research in all the different parts of the canon. How much more difficult for the minister, rabbi, student, or interested layperson! Herein lies the importance of bibliographies and in particular this series—IBR Bibliographies.

Bibliographies help guide students to works relevant to their research interests. They cut down the time needed to locate materials, thus providing the researcher with more time to read, assimilate, and write. These benefits are especially true for the IBR Bibliographies. First, the series is conveniently laid out along the major divisions of the canon, with four volumes planned on the Old Testament, six on the New Testament, and four on methodology (see page 2). Each volume will contain approximately five hundred entries, arranged under various topics to allow for ease of reference. Since the possible entries far exceed this number, the compiler of each volume must select the more important and helpful works for inclusion. Furthermore, the entries are briefly annotated in order to inform the reader about their contents more specifically, once again giving guidance to the appropriate material and saving time by preventing the all too typical "wild goose chase" in the library.

One of the problems with published bibliographies in the past is that they are soon out of date. The development of computer-based publishing has changed this, however, and it is the plan of the Institute for Biblical Research and Baker Book House to publish updates of each volume about every five years.

Since the series is designed primarily for American and British students, the emphasis is on works written in English, with a five-percent limit on titles not translated into English. Fortunately, a number of the most important foreign-language works have been translated into English, and wherever this is the case this information is included along with the original publication data. Again keeping in mind the needs of the student, we have decided to list the English translation before the original title (for chronological purposes, the titles are arranged according to the dates of their original publication).

These bibliographies are presented under the sponsorship of the Institute for Biblical Research (IBR), an organization of evangelical Christian scholars with specialties in both Old and New Testaments and their ancillary disciplines. The IBR has met annually since 1970; its name and constitution were adopted in 1973. Besides its annual meetings (normally held the evening and morning prior to the annual meeting of the Society of Biblical Literature), the institute publishes a journal, *Bulletin for Biblical Research,* and conducts regional study groups on various biblical themes in several areas of the United States and Canada. The Institute for Biblical Research encourages and fosters scholarly research among its members, all of whom are at a level to qualify for a university lectureship. Finally, the IBR and the series editor extend their thanks to Baker Book House for its efforts to bring this series to publication. In particular, we would like to thank David Aiken for his wise guidance in giving shape to the project.

Tremper Longman III
Westminster Theological Seminary

Author's Preface

A volume of this size does not permit anything approaching an exhaustive survey of the literature on wisdom and poetry in the OT. It is assumed that anyone engaged in research on these topics will consult the standard bibliographic works (e.g., *Religion Index One, Religion Index Two, Old Testament Abstracts*) and general introductions to the OT. Also, in an effort to save more space for articles and essays, only a very few commentaries have been included in this volume. Anyone interested in surveying the commentaries should consult Tremper Longman III's *Old Testament Commentary Survey* (Baker, 1995). This work is currently in its second edition with periodic updates expected.

It should be pointed out at the outset that a fair degree of overlap is to be expected among the sections in this volume. This is unavoidable. There are a number of works, for example, in the General Introduction to Wisdom section (§1.2.1), that treat the individual wisdom books, but still, for a number of other reasons, deserve to be classified in the General Introduction section. The point, therefore, is that works that treat Job, for example, are not restricted to §3 but may be found in §1 as well. One specific example is #398, A. Cook's *The Root of the Thing: A Study of Job and the Song of Songs*, which treats the dramatic form of both Job and the Song of Songs. This book is found in §3.5, but would certainly be relevant in §7 as well, but a decision had to be made. Another area of overlap concerns the anthologies and introductions. Many specific topics of research are addressed more generally in these works, and, hence, should not be neglected.

Occasionally, a quotation is provided from an article that was reprinted in a collected volume. At times, the page numbers correspond to the pagination as it appears in the collected volume rather than its original publication. This should cause no confusion.

I would like to take this opportunity to thank the staff at the Montgomery Library, Westminster Theological Seminary, for their help in securing quickly, and without the benefit of a computerized library system, many of the sources represented in this volume, either through interlibrary loan or tracking down negligent borrowers. In particular, I would like to mention the indefatigable assistance of Grace Mullen, Assistant Librarian and Archivist, and Gail Barker, Circulation Librarian. Tremper Longman, series editor, is both a friend and colleague. His advice has proved valuable throughout. My current research assistants, John Makujina and Jennifer Dowda, were most helpful in the final stages of this project by proofreading the final draft. As always, the author assumes all responsibility for any mistakes that may have run this gauntlet of proofreaders. I would also like to thank Jesse Buck, my research assistant at the early stages of this project, for his legwork and energy. Jesse has since moved on (perhaps wisely) to other, nonacademic, pastures. I trust that his work on this volume was not the precipitating factor.

Abbreviations

ANE   Ancient Near East(ern)
BETL   Bibliotheca ephemeridum theologicarum lovaniensum
Bib   Biblica
BSac   Bibliotheca Sacra
BTB   Biblical Theology Bulletin
BZAW   Beihefte zur Zeitschrift für die alttestamentlich
          Wissenschaft
CBQ   Catholic Biblical Quarterly
CBQMS   Catholic Biblical Quarterly Monograph Series
HAR   Hebrew Annual Review
HUCA   Hebrew Union College Annual
Int   Interpretation
JAAR   Journal of the American Academy of Religion
JBL   Journal of Biblical Literature
JQR   Jewish Quarterly Review
JSOT   Journal for the Study of the Old Testament
JSOTSup   Journal for the Study of the Old Testament Supplement
JSS   Journal of Semitic Studies
RB   Revue biblique
SBLDS   Society of Biblical Literature Dissertation Series

TBT	*The Bible Today*
TynBul	*Tyndale Bulletin*
VT	*Vetus Testamentum*
VTSup	Vetus Testamentum Supplement
ZAW	*Zeitschrift für die alttestamentlich Wissenschaft*

Part 1

Wisdom

1. Wisdom in Ancient Israel

Wisdom scholarship has blossomed over the past generation or two. Whereas the previous history of OT study has tended to focus on such familiar topics as cult, covenant, or Heilsgeschichte, wisdom literature has lately been given more detailed attention, particularly concerning its origins and ANE influences, social setting, theology, and the presence of wisdom in the Old Testament outside the wisdom corpus. The recognition of the importance of wisdom during the Second Temple period, particularly its relationship to Hellenism and its impact on the nature of biblical interpretation during this period, has given some impetus to the reexamination of the nature of wisdom in the OT proper.

1.1 Anthologies

Anthologies are helpful during the early stages of research. The breadth of issues typically addressed will often introduce the reader to some of the broader issues involved in researching a particular topic. Anthologies are also valuable bibliographic sources. Many of the essays contained in the following works are annotated separetely under the appropriate headings.

1   M. Noth and D. W. Thomas (eds.). *Wisdom in Israel and in the Ancient Near East: Presented to Professor Harold Henry Rowley.* VTSup 3. Leiden: E. J. Brill, 1955.

     Twenty-two essays written by prominent scholars in honor of H. H. Rowley covering a variety of biblical and ANE wisdom topics. Essays written in English, German, and French.

2   P. Skehan. *Studies in Israelite Poetry and Wisdom.* CBQMS, 1. Washington, D.C.: Catholic Biblical Association, 1971.

     Collection of twenty-six of the author's previously published essays on biblical and apocryphal wisdom literature. Also includes ten of the author's reviews of other scholarly works on wisdom topics.

3   J. L. Crenshaw (ed.). *Studies in Ancient Israelite Wisdom.* New York: KTAV, 1976.

     Includes twenty-seven essays by various authors, all previously published, under five headings: wisdom's ANE setting, thought structure, theology, literary heritage, and intersection of wisdom and the rest of the OT. Helpful prolegomenon by the editor provides an introduction to the world of wisdom scholarship. Contains English translations of important foreign works.

4   J. G. Gammie et al. (eds.). *Israelite Wisdom: Theological and Literary Essays in Honor of Samuel Terrien.* Missoula: Scholars, 1978.

     Eighteen essays grouped under the following categories: the meaning and study of Israelite wisdom; wisdom and the prophets; provenance, ethics, and theology; Ecclesiasticus; wisdom and apocalyptic.

5   M. Gilbert (ed.). *La Sagesse de l'Ancien Testament.* BETL, 51. Leuven: Leuven University Press, 1979.

     Essays in English, German, and French on a variety of topics concerning biblical and apocryphal wisdom books, and the influence of wisdom elsewhere in the OT.

6   K. G. Hoglund et al. (eds.). *The Listening Heart: Essays in Wisdom and the Psalms in Honor of Roland E. Murphy, O. Carm.* JSOTSup 58. Sheffield: JSOT, 1987.

     Fifteen essays related to biblical and extrabiblical wisdom, and to various issues surrounding Psalms.

7   J. G. Gammie and L. G. Perdue (eds.). *The Sage in Israel and the Ancient Near East.* Winona Lake, Ind.: Eisenbrauns, 1990.

Thirty-six brief introductory essays written specifically for this volume by top scholars in the field. Divided into six categories: ANE literature, social functions, OT wisdom literature, other OT literature, post–OT literature (including Hellenistic literature, Pseudepigrapha, Apocrypha, Qumran, NT, rabbinic writings), and the sage's symbolic universe. Includes an extensive bibliography and indexes of modern and classical authors, ANE texts, and biblical and extrabiblical texts.

8   L. G. Perdue et al. (eds.). *In Search of Wisdom: Essays in Memory of John G. Gammie*. Louisville: Westminster/John Knox, 1993.
Collection of fifteen introductory essays on wisdom in the OT (1–7), in the Apocrypha (8–9), its relationship to apocalypticism (10), and in the NT (11–15).

9   J. Day, R. P. Gordon, and H. G. M. Williamson (eds.). *Wisdom in Ancient Israel: Essays in Honor of J. A. Emerton*. Cambridge: Cambridge University Press, 1996.
Twenty original essays divided into three categories: (1) ANE setting (Egyptian, Babylonian, Ahiqar); (2) OT and apocryphal texts; (3) themes (miscellaneous issues, including schools, personification, Qumran, theology).

1.2. Introductions

The works contained under this heading, as distinct from anthologies, are by one author, either of book length or essays contained in other volumes. Many contain chapters or sections that pertain specifically to some of the other categories outlined below, including the individual wisdom books.

1.2.1. History of Scholarship

These works have as their primary focus the history of scholarship. This is not to say, however, that this issue is not treated in the other introductions in some form.

10   R. E. Murphy. "Assumptions and Problems in Old Testament Wisdom Research." *CBQ* 29 (1967): 102–12.
Outlines six problematic areas for future study of wisdom literature: origins, extent, the sages, the mentality of the sages, wisdom and history, wisdom personified.

11   R. E. Murphy. "Form Criticism and Wisdom Literature." *CBQ* 31 (1969): 475–83.

      Briefly reviews efforts to apply form criticism to wisdom literature, emphasizing the problems and major issues involved in determining wisdom's life setting.

12   R. E. Murphy. "The Interpretation of Old Testament Wisdom Literature." *Int* 23 (1969): 289–301.
      Reviews briefly the major trends in the history of modern wisdom scholarship. Treats three questions that help the reader in better interpreting the wisdom corpus: the experiential nature of wisdom, the reinterpretation of proverbs within the Bible, wisdom-like material outside wisdom literature.

13   R. B. Y. Scott. "The Study of the Wisdom Literature." *Int* 24 (1970): 20–45.
      Survey of the growing field of wisdom research, especially scholarship concerning wisdom in its ANE setting.

14   R. E. Clements. "Interpreting the Wisdom Literature." Pp. 99–117 in Clements' *One Hundred Years of Old Testament Interpretation*. Philadelphia: Westminster, 1976.
      Overview of major themes in the history of wisdom scholarship.

15   J. A. Emerton. "Wisdom." Pp. 214–37 in *Tradition and Interpretation*. Edited by G. W. Anderson. Oxford: Clarendon, 1979.
      Survey of scholarship on six issues concerning modern wisdom scholarship: non-Israelite wisdom literature; wisdom literature and OT theology; wisdom elements in the OT outside the specific wisdom books; literary problems in Proverbs; personification of wisdom; the book of Job.

16   R. E. Murphy. "Hebrew Wisdom." *Journal of the American Oriental Society* 101 (1981): 21–34.
      Survey of the scholarship on the biblical and apocryphal wisdom books, and major issues involved in the study of wisdom literature. Contains bibliography.

17   D. Bergant. *What Are They Saying about Wisdom Literature?* New York: Paulist, 1984.
      Overview of current state of scholarship on Proverbs, Job, Qoheleth, Ben Sira, and Wisdom, as well as the definition and setting of wisdom and wisdom influence elsewhere in the OT.

18   J. L. Crenshaw. "Wisdom Literature: Retrospect and Prospect." Pp. 161–78 in *Of Prophets' Visions and the Wisdom of the Sages: Essays in Honour of R. Norman Whybray on His Seventieth*

Birthday. Edited by H. A. McKay and D. J. A. Clines. JSOTSup 162. Sheffield: JSOT, 1993.

Overview of recent research on wisdom literature: social setting, discourse, and concept of God.

19 W. P. Brown. *Character in Crisis: A Fresh Approach to the Wisdom Literature of the Old Testament.* Grand Rapids: Eerdmans, 1996.

Purpose of biblical wisdom literature is to form moral character within the context of family and community security and identity. Includes discussions on Proverbs 1:1–7, Job, and Ecclesiastes.

1.2.2. General Introduction

20 J. F. Genung. *The Hebrew Literature of Wisdom in the Light of Today.* Boston: Houghton Mifflin, 1906.

Introduction to the wisdom literature of the OT (Proverbs, Job, Ecclesiastes), Apocrypha (Ben Sira, Wisdom of Solomon), and NT (Gospels, James). Includes two opening chapters: an introduction to wisdom and the *mœßœl* form.

21 H. Ranston. *The Old Testament Wisdom Books and Their Teaching.* London: Epworth, 1930.

General introduction to and outline of the teachings of Proverbs, Job, Song of Songs, and Ecclesiastes.

22 O. S. Rankin. *Israel's Wisdom Literature: Its Bearing on Theology and the History of Religion.* Edinburgh: T. & T. Clark, 1936.

Study of wisdom literature engaging both its historical development in Israel and its theological content. Major topics of discussion include immortality, personification of wisdom, reward and retribution, and creation. Includes discussions on deuterocanonical and NT wisdom. Speaks of the "debt which Judaism and Christianity owe to the Wisdom-school" (p. viii).

23 W. A. Baumgartner. "The Wisdom Literature." Pp. 210–37 in *The Old Testament and Modern Study.* Edited by H. H. Rowley. Oxford: Clarendon, 1951.

Analysis of biblical and apocryphal wisdom literature. Stresses ANE background.

24 R. E. Murphy. *Seven Books of Wisdom.* Milwaukee: Bruce, 1960.

Introductory chapters discussing biblical (Proverbs, Psalms, Job, Song of Songs, Ecclesiastes) and apocryphal (Ben Sira, Wis-

dom of Solomon) wisdom. Also includes opening chapter on
the nature of Hebrew poetry and a concluding chapter sum-
marizing the nature of wisdom in the OT.

25   H. W. Robinson. "Revelation in 'Wisdom.'" Pp. 231–61 in *Inspi-
ration and Revelation in the Old Testament*. Oxford: Clarendon,
1962.
Wisdom in its ANE setting; ethics (schools and teaching);
theology (faith versus experience, theodicy, personification of
wisdom).

26   R. E. Murphy. *Introduction to the Wisdom Literature of the Old
Testament*. Collegeville, Minn.: Liturgical, 1965.
Discussion of four basic areas of wisdom research: its poetic
form, its origins, extrabiblical parallels, and the varieties of
and developments in wisdom literature of the OT.

27   J. Wood. *Wisdom Literature: An Introduction*. London: Duckworth, 1967.
Popular overview of wisdom in the ANE, the OT, Pseudepigrapha, Apocrypha, and the NT. Appendix on hypostasis of
wisdom.

28   G. von Rad. *Wisdom in Israel*. Translated by J. D. Martin.
Nashville: Abingdon, 1972. Original Title: *Weisheit in Israel*.
Neukirchener Verlag, 1970.
Classic, comprehensive study that addresses under various
headings the questions of the origin, literary expressions, and
theology of wisdom in the OT primarily, but also during the
intertestamental period. Point of departure for serious study
of wisdom. Emphasizes wisdom's didactic function in the
royal court. Wisdom gave rise to apocalyptic.

29   R. B. Y. Scott. *The Way of Wisdom in the Old Testament*. New
York: Macmillan, 1971.
Introduction to wisdom literature organized not according to
the biblical books but issues relevant to the proper understanding of wisdom. Discusses wisdom's international context, types of proverbs, wisdom in stories and word pictures,
its relation to prophecy, wisdom in revolt (Job, Agur, and
Qoheleth).

30   J. L. Crenshaw. "Wisdom." Pp. 225–64 in *Old Testament Form
Criticism*. Edited by J. H. Hayes. San Antonio: Trinity University Press, 1974.

Discussion of eight categories of biblical wisdom literature (complete with bibliography for each): proverb (*māšāl*), riddle (*ḥîdâ*), fable and allegory, hymn and prayer, *Streitgespräch* or dialogue, confession (autobiographical narrative), lists (onomastica), didactic poetry, and narrative.

31 R. L. Wilken (ed.). *Aspects of Wisdom in Judaism and Early Christianity.* University of Notre Dame Center for the Study of Judaism and Christianity, 1. Notre Dame, Ind.: University of Notre Dame, 1975.

Seven introductory essays treating the influence of wisdom on the NT. Essays on Gospels, christological hymns, Paul and Hellenistic-Jewish wisdom, wisdom and midrash, Philo, early Christianity, and Christian asceticism.

32 J. L. Crenshaw. *Old Testament Wisdom: An Introduction.* Atlanta: John Knox/London: SCM, 1981.

Introduction to wisdom in the Bible and Apocrypha. Includes chapter on Egyptian and Mesopotamian literature.

33 R. E. Murphy. *Wisdom Literature: Job, Proverbs, Ruth, Canticles, Ecclesiastes, and Esther.* The Forms of Old Testament Literature, 13. Grand Rapids: Eerdmans, 1981.

Form-critical analysis of these six biblical books. Includes introductory chapter on basic wisdom genres.

34 J. L. Crenshaw. "The Wisdom Literature." Pp. 369–407 in *The Hebrew Bible and Its Modern Interpreters.* Edited by D. G. Knight and G. M. Tucker. Philadelphia: Fortress/ Chico, Calif.: Scholars, 1985.

Brief introduction to wisdom literature, including extrabiblical parallels, its influence in the Hebrew Bible, and modern approaches. Also discusses the literary forms, theology, and contemporary approaches to Proverbs, Ecclesiastes, and Job. Concludes with suggestions for further study.

35 D. Kidner. *An Introduction to Wisdom Literature: The Wisdom of Proverbs, Job and Ecclesiastes.* Downers Grove: InterVarsity, 1985.

Basic introduction to each of the three biblical books as well as summary and evaluation of scholarly debate on various points of interest for each. Includes three appendixes on wisdom in the ANE, Ecclesiasticus, and the Wisdom of Solomon.

36 R. E. Clements. "Wisdom." Pp. 67–83 in *It Is Written: Scripture Citing Scripture: Essays in Honour of Barnabas Lindars, SSF.*

Edited by D. A. Carson and H. G. M. Williamson. Cambridge: Cambridge University Press, 1988.

> Discussion of "three main areas where . . . wisdom teaching developed a direct and positive interest in the emergent biblical tradition at a surprisingly early stage" (p. 68): creation, development of the concept of Torah, and Solomon as founder of the Israelite wisdom tradition.

37   R. E. Murphy. *The Tree of Life: An Exploration of Biblical Wisdom Literature*. Anchor Bible Reference Library. New York: Doubleday, 1992.

> Introductory chapters on Proverbs, Job, Qoheleth, Ben Sira, and the Wisdom of Solomon. Also includes chapters on wisdom's "echoes" throughout the OT, the intersection of wisdom and theology, and the personification of wisdom (Lady Wisdom) in the various wisdom books.

38   D. K. Berry. *An Introduction to Wisdom and Poetry of the Old Testament*. Nashville: Broadman & Holman, 1995.

> Comprehensive introduction to wisdom in general, the wisdom literature of the Bible and the ANE, poetry, and the poetical books of the OT. Includes glossary of terms and brief bibliographies of wisdom, poetry, history of interpretation, and ANE literature.

39   J. Blenkinsopp. "The Sage." Pp. 9–65 in *Sage, Priest, Prophet: Religious and Intellectual Leadership in Ancient Israel*. Louisville: Westminster/John Knox, 1995.

> Role of the sage in sustaining, transmitting, and transforming ancient Israelite religion.

1.3. Origins and ANE Influence

The origins of Israelite wisdom is a topic that has exercised scholars for some time, particularly in light of the existence of similar traditions evinced in the writings of Israel's neighbors. Many of these ANE traditions are not only very similar to what we find in the biblical wisdom corpus but are certainly older as well. Not surprisingly, such factors have led scholars to investigate more closely Israel's own wisdom tradition, that is, to what extent the trajectories of Israelite wisdom were influenced, if not determined, by these surrounding forces. In the final analysis, it seems certain that Israel's wisdom tradition as a historical phenomenon cannot be understood in isolation from the broader wisdom influences of the world in which the Israelite sages thought and wrote.

1.3.1. General Studies

40 D. B. MacDonald. *The Hebrew Philosophical Genius: A Vindication*. Princeton, N.J.: Princeton University Press, 1936. Reprinted: New York: Russell & Russell, 1965.

Biblical and postbiblical Jewish wisdom (Hebrew philosophy) is rooted in Israel's Palestinian environment and is not dependent on (although not unaffected by) later Greek influence.

41 H. Ringgren. *Word and Wisdom: Studies in the Hypostatization of Divine Qualities and Functions in the Ancient Near East*. Lund: Ohlssons, 1947.

Contrary to the evolutionary model of religious development in the ancient world, monotheism is the "primitive religion" (p. 7). Polytheism in Egyptian, "Sumero-Accadian," and West Semitic religions is a derivative of monotheism and results from the hypostatization of divine qualities (e.g., wisdom) and functions, as well as from the personification of certain cult names. Israelite religion and Islam resisted this tendency.

42 R. Marcus. "On Biblical Hypostases of Wisdom." *HUCA* 23 (1950–51): 157–71.

Reviews the argument of H. Ringgren (#41), that the hypostatization of divine qualities often leads from monotheism to polytheism. The reason Wisdom did not become fully personified in Israel is because of late biblical, antimythological influence.

43 A. Alt. "Solomonic Wisdom." Translated by D. A. Knight. Pp. 102–12 in *Studies in Ancient Israelite Wisdom*. Edited by J. L. Crenshaw. New York: KTAV, 1976. Original Title: "Die Wiesheit Salomos." *Theologische Literaturzeitung* 76 (1951): 139–44.

Argues for a special *Gattung* of nature wisdom attributable to Solomon but which became "almost totally suppressed by the mass of wisdom literature about human life" (p. 104). Israelite nature wisdom has likely literary ties with Babylonian and Egyptian "enumerative science," a form that Solomon transformed by expanding the enumerations to whole proverbs and songs.

44 R. B. Y. Scott. "Solomon and the Beginnings of Wisdom in Israel." Pp. 262–79 in *Wisdom in Israel and in the Ancient Near East:*

Presented to Professor Harold Henry Rowley. Edited by M. Noth and D. W. Thomas. VTSup 3. Leiden: E. J. Brill, 1955. Reprinted in J. L. Crenshaw's *Studies in Ancient Israelite Wisdom.* New York: KTAV, 1976, pp. 84–101.

> First Kings 3:12–13, which connects Solomon with the origins of Israelite wisdom, is "post-exilic in date and legendary in character." The true point of origin should be sought in Hezekiah (Prov. 25:1), who deliberately cultivated the Solomonic tradition "as part of his grandiose plans to restore the vanished glories of Solomon's kingdom" (p. 101).

45   W. O. E. Oesterley. "The Wisdom Literature—A Sage among His People." Pp. 57–80 in *Judaism and Christianity.* Vol. 1: *The Age of Transition.* New York: KTAV, 1969.

> Argues for biblical wisdom literature as a codification of originally oral tradition, since the masses were unable to read. Wisdom emphasizes the spoken word, friendship, and other commonalities.

1.3.2. ANE Wisdom Traditions

1.3.2.1. General

46   J. Pedersen. "Wisdom and Immortality." Pp. 238–46 in *Wisdom in Israel and in the Ancient Near East: Presented to Professor Harold Henry Rowley.* Edited by M. Noth and D. W. Thomas. VTSup 3. Leiden: E. J. Brill, 1955.

> The interplay of wisdom and immortality in the ANE vis-à-vis humanity's kinship with the gods and the ultimate completion of that kinship through immortality.

47   F. C. Fensham. "Widow, Orphan, and the Poor in Ancient Near Eastern Legal and Wisdom Literature." *Journal of Near Eastern Studies* 21 (1962): 129–39. Reprinted in J. L. Crenshaw's *Studies in Ancient Israelite Wisdom.* New York: KTAV, 1976, pp. 161–71.

> Compares the treatment of the disenfranchised in Mesopotamia, Egypt, Ugarit, and the OT. The evidence shows that it was common policy throughout the ancient world for the king to offer protection to these people as a divine prerogative.

48   J. A. Loader. "Relativity in Near Eastern Wisdom." Pp. 49–58 in *Studies in Wisdom Literature.* Edited by W. C. van Wyk. *Ou-Testamentiese Werkgemeenskap in Suid-Afrika,* 15–16. Potchesfstroom: Pro Rege, 1972–73.

Wisdom is relative insofar as it remains connected to reality. When wisdom retreats from real-life situations and attempts to make absolute pronouncements (e.g., Job's friends), it stagnates into a "doctrine" of retribution.

49 L. Kalugula. *The Wise King: Studies in Royal Wisdom as Divine Revelation in the Old Testament and Its Environment.* Coniectanae biblica, Old Testament, 15. Lund: CWK Gleerup, 1980.
Study of relevant biblical and ANE texts to investigate (1) the proper definition of wisdom; (2) gods who were considered wise; (3) kings who claimed to possess wisdom; (4) how wise kings applied their wisdom.

1.3.2.2. Egypt

50 W. O. E. Oesterley. "The 'Teaching of Amen-em-ope' and the Old Testament." *ZAW* 45 (1927): 9–24.
The religious posture represented in this Egyptian text is unique to Egyptian literature, and finds its closest parallel in OT wisdom. The religious and ethical stance of this text is more likely the result of Israelite influence than vice-versa.

51 W. O. E. Oesterley. *The Wisdom of Egypt and the Old Testament in the Light of the Newly Discovered Teaching of Amenemope.* New York and Toronto: Macmillan, 1927.
Expansion of the author's *ZAW* article (#50). Overview of scholarship on the teaching of *Amenemope* and its contents. Comparison to Proverbs, Deuteronomy, and Psalms. Egyptian and Israelite traditions borrowed from each other.

52 E. Würthwein. "Egyptian Wisdom and the Old Testament." Translated by B. W. Kovacs. Pp. 113–33 in *Studies in Ancient Israelite Wisdom.* Edited by J. L. Crenshaw. New York: KTAV, 1976. Original Title: "Die Weisheit Ägyptens und das Alte Testament; Rede zur Rektoratsübergabe am 29. November 1958." In *Schriften der Philips-Universität Marburg.* Vol. 6. Marburg: N. G. Elwert Verlag, 1960.
Israelite wisdom is not a product of Israel itself, but a witness to Israel's encounter with other cultures. Proverbs, Ecclesiastes, and Job represent diverse responses within Israel over the degree to which such foreign influence should be appropriated.

53 B. Gemser. "The Instructions of 'Onchsheshonqy and Biblical Wisdom Literature." Pp. 102–28 in *Congress Volume: Oxford,*

1959. VTSup 7. Leiden: E. J. Brill, 1960. Reprinted in J. L. Crenshaw's *Studies in Ancient Israelite Wisdom.* New York: KTAV, 1976, pp. 134–60.

Discusses in some detail various scholarly issues surrounding the *Instructions of 'Onchsheshonqy* in particular, and briefly compares this Egyptian document to biblical wisdom.

54   G. E. Bryce. *A Legacy of Wisdom: The Egyptian Contribution to the Wisdom of Israel.* Lewisburg, Pa.: Bucknell University Press, 1979.

Israelite wisdom "adapted Egyptian ideas, proverbs, and literary forms in the development of their own traditions" (p. 87). In doing so, these Egyptian elements were adapted, assimilated, and integrated into Israelite culture via the royal court.

55   R. J. Williams. "The Sages of Egypt in the Light of Recent Scholarship." *Journal of the American Oriental Society* 101 (1981): 1–20.

Introductory survey of scholarship since 1960 on Egyptian background for Israelite wisdom.

56   R. J. Williams. "The Functions of the Sage in the Egyptian Royal Court." Pp. 95–98 in *The Sage in Israel and the Ancient Near East.* Edited by J. G. Gammie and L. G. Perdue. Winona Lake, Ind.: Eisenbrauns, 1990.

Very brief annotated list of the Egyptian sage's various royal functions. Includes magician/sorcerer, dream interpreter, advisor, diplomat, problem-solver, physician, entertainer, government official, counselor.

57   R. J. Williams. "The Sage in Egyptian Literature." Pp. 19–30 in *The Sage in Israel and the Ancient Near East.* Edited by J. G. Gammie and L. G. Perdue. Winona Lake, Ind.: Eisenbrauns, 1990.

Reviews the profound influence the Egyptian sages had on the development of their culture, particularly the invention of the hieroglyphic writing system, which "made possible the development of a literary élite into whose hands the government of the land was entrusted" (p. 19).

58   N. Shupak. *Where Can Wisdom Be Found? The Sage's Language in the Bible and in Ancient Egyptian Literature.* Orbis biblicus et orietalis, 130. Fribourg: Fribourg University Press; Göttingen: Vandenhoeck und Ruprecht, 1993.

Comparison of Israelite and Egyptian wisdom vocabulary. Hebrew books discussed include Job, Proverbs, Ecclesiastes, wisdom psalms, and Ben Sira. Origin of Israelite wisdom is instruction in the royal court (see §1.4).

1.3.2.3. Ugarit

59 J. Khanjian. "Wisdom." Pp. 371–400 in *Ras Shamra Parallels*, II. Edited by L. Fisher. Analecta orientalia, 50. Rome: Pontifical Biblical Institute, 1975.

Comparative study of the similar motifs, literary phrases, formulas, and word pairs in Ugaritic and OT wisdom texts. Fifty-two parallels are discussed.

60 D. E. Smith. "Wisdom Genres in RS 22.439." Pp. 215–47 in *Ras Shamra Parallels, II*. Edited by L. Fisher. Analecta orientalia 50. Rome: Pontifical Biblical Institute, 1975.

Eight Ugaritic texts and their parallels in OT wisdom. "The sages of Ugarit and Israel worked within a common tradition, they used common structures and structural devices in their teaching" (p. 218).

61 A. Caquot. "Israelite Perceptions of Wisdom and Strength in Light of the Ras Shamra Texts." Pp. 25–33 in *Israelite Wisdom: Theological and Literary Essays in Honor of Samuel Terrien*. Edited by J. G. Gammie et al. Missoula: Scholars, 1978.

Wisdom and strength both function in the lives of people and societies. The proper balance between them is achieved when strength serves wisdom. In Israel, "the one true God must simultaneously assume the role of the wise and of the strong" (p. 29).

62 L. R. Mack-Fisher. "The Scribe (and Sage) in the Royal Court at Ugarit." Pp. 109–15 in *The Sage in Israel and the Ancient Near East*. Edited by J. G. Gammie and L. G. Perdue. Winona Lake, Ind.: Eisenbrauns, 1990.

Partial list of scribes and the kings under whom they worked with explanatory comments on some of the scribes.

63 L. R. Mack-Fisher. "A Survey and Reading Guide to the Didactic Literature of Ugarit: Prolegomenon to a Study on the Sage." Pp. 67–80 in *The Sage in Israel and the Ancient Near East*. Edited by J. G. Gammie and L. G. Perdue. Winona Lake, Ind.: Eisenbrauns, 1990.

Provides a representative list of didactic texts found at Ugarit. Focuses on the actual didactic corpus rather than the author/sage that may have been responsible for the work.

1.3.2.4. Other

64 W. F. Albright. "Some Canaanite-Phoenician Sources of Hebrew
Wisdom." Pp. 1–15 in *Wisdom in Israel and in the Ancient Near
East: Presented to Professor Harold Henry Rowley*. Edited by M.
Noth and D. W. Thomas. VTSup 3. Leiden: E. J. Brill, 1955.
Biblical wisdom books "draw heavily on traditional Canaan-
ite-Phoenician didactic sources" (p. 4), although they are "sat-
urated with Israelite theism and morality" (p. 13).

65 G. E. Bryce. "Omen-Wisdom in Ancient Israel." *JBL* 94 (1975):
19–37.
Similarity between OT proverbs and Babylonian omen-
wisdom. Priestly elements are evident in the composition and
collection of OT proverbs. Hence, there are points of contact
between priestly and wisdom elements (e.g., creation, universalism).

66 J. G. Gammie. "The Sage in Hellenistic Royal Courts." Pp.
147–53 in *The Sage in Israel and the Ancient Near East*. Edited
by J. G. Gammie and L. G. Perdue. Winona Lake, Ind.: Eisenbrauns, 1990.
The role of the sage in Hellenism was held by both theoreti-
cal philosophers (Peripatetics, Stoics, Epicureans) and coun-
selors/confidants of the kings.

67 S. N. Kramer. "The Sage in Sumerian Literature: A Composite
Portrait." Pp. 31–44 in *The Sage in Israel and the Ancient Near
East*. Edited by J. G. Gammie and L. G. Perdue. Winona Lake,
Ind.: Eisenbrauns, 1990.
Discussion of the role of the Sumerian sage in education, the
cult, and the palace.

68 J. R. Russell. "The Sage in Ancient Iranian Literature." Pp. 81–92
in *The Sage in Israel and the Ancient Near East*. Edited by J. G.
Gammie and L. G. Perdue. Winona Lake, Ind.: Eisenbrauns, 1990.
Focuses on the prophet-sage Zarathustra. Includes brief discussion on the various activities of the Iranian sage (dream
interpretation, maker/compiler of maxims, education, legal
function) as well as brief remarks on the impact of Persian
wisdom on Christianity, Judaism, and Greco-Roman religions.

69 J. R. Russell. "Sages and Scribes at the Courts of Ancient Iran."
Pp. 141–46 in *The Sage in Israel and the Ancient Near East*.

Edited by J. G. Gammie and L. G. Perdue. Winona Lake, Ind.: Eisenbrauns, 1990.

Outlines the role of sages in Iranian political life, including clerical and scribal tasks, function as physicians.

70   R. F. G. Sweet. "The Sage in Akkadian Literature: A Philological Study." Pp. 45–65 in *The Sage in Israel and the Ancient Near East*. Edited by J. G. Gammie and L. G. Perdue. Winona Lake, Ind.: Eisenbrauns, 1990.

Analysis of the vocabulary of wisdom in Akkadian literature. Kingly wisdom is identified with reverence for the gods (i.e., not an intellectual concept). Wisdom vocabulary also applies to "professions that required an obvious or special skill" (p. 65). What is missing is the identification of the learned class with wisdom.

71   R. F. G. Sweet. "The Sage in Mesopotamian Palaces and Royal Courts." Pp. 99–107 in *The Sage in Israel and the Ancient Near East*. Edited by J. G. Gammie and L. G. Perdue. Winona Lake, Ind.: Eisenbrauns, 1990.

Identification of wisdom with the wise rule of the king, but still dependent in part on the delegation of responsibility to subordinates skilled in various areas (science, technology, crafts). Role of scribes and diviners.

1.4. Social Setting

Where in Israel's social structure did wisdom find its home? Who was responsible for passing on the wisdom tradition? Various answers to these questions have been given, including the royal court, the family, schools, and the temple. In recent years, wisdom influence has been thought to embrace a variety of social settings rather than simply one or another.

72   R. Gordis. "The Social Background of Wisdom Literature." *HUCA* 18 (1944): 77–118. Reprinted in *Poets, Prophets, and Sages*. Bloomington: Indiana University Press, 1971, pp. 160–97.

The political, social, religious, and moral points of view expressed in wisdom literature reflect an upper-class social setting, a setting that later developed into Sadduceeism.

73   J. W. Gaspar. *Social Ideas in the Wisdom Literature of the Old Testament*. Studies in Sacred Theology, 2/8. Washington, D.C.: Catholic University of America Press, 1947.

Treats views on marriage, father, wife, children, education, and the social function of the community in OT wisdom literature. "The teaching of the sages is essentially a moral teaching, which is based on wisdom, which is based on God" (p. xiv).

74 N. W. Porteous. "Royal Wisdom." Pp. 247–61 in *Wisdom in Israel and in the Ancient Near East: Presented to Professor Harold Henry Rowley.* VTSup 3. Edited by M. Noth and D. W. Thomas. Leiden: E. J. Brill, 1955.

Although wisdom in Israel became 'democratized' to govern everyday life, there also continued alongside this the conviction that wisdom was an especial requirement of the king. Includes discussion of OT, ANE, apocryphal, and NT texts.

75 W. H. Gispen. "The Wise Men in Israel." *Free University Quarterly* 5, no. 1 (1957): 1–18.

Investigation of biblical and extrabiblical data as to whether there was a separate class of wise men in Israel who held a special office in the court. The wise man was primarily involved in education of the young.

76 R. N. Whybray. *The Intellectual Tradition in the Old Testament.* BZAW, 135. Berlin: Walter de Gruyter, 1974.

Analysis of Israel's wisdom tradition focusing on terminology, in particular, the root *ḥkm* There is no OT evidence for a special class of wisdom writers in ancient Israel. Israel's intellectual tradition did not have institutional moorings. Includes list of wisdom texts.

77 J. P. J. Oliver. "Schools and Wisdom Literature." *Journal of Northwest Semitic Languages* 4 (1975): 49–60.

Evidence shows that schools did exist in the ANE. "Moreover, wisdom literature constituted a major part in the curriculum of these schools and was most probably regarded as highly suitable material for the training of scribes" (p. 59).

78 L. G. Perdue. "Liminality as a Social Setting for Wisdom Instructions." *ZAW* 93 (1981): 114–26.

Interacting with the social-anthropological work of V. Turner, the author concludes that the social setting for wisdom instructions "may be best described in terms of liminality which is a phase within the 'rites of passage' that accompany status elevation" (p. 125). The father's function in instruction is to elevate the son's status to "father."

79 J. D. Pleins. "Poverty in the Social World of the Wise." *JSOT* 37 (1987): 61–78.

> Wisdom is an urban-elite phenomenon, as an investigation of wisdom's ambivalent view of poverty shows. Such a view of poverty differs from that of the prophetic literature.

80 J. K. Wiles. "Wisdom and Kingship in Israel." *Asian Journal of Theology* 1 (1987): 55–70.

> In Israel, "wisdom functioned as a theological underpinning of kingship" (p. 65). Seen in the king's role as guardian of justice, mediator of blessing, ruler over other nations, and mediator between Yahweh and the wise.

81 R. N. Whybray. "The Social World of the Wisdom Writers." Pp. 227–50 in *The World of Ancient Israel: Sociological, Anthropological and Political Perspectives*. Edited by R. N. Clements. Cambridge: Cambridge University Press, 1989.

> Brief outline of the biblical wisdom books, in which "we encounter a series of quite different styles and approaches which reflect widely different intellectual and social worlds" (p. 229).

82 W. Brueggemann. "The Social Significance of Solomon as a Patron of Wisdom." Pp. 117–32 in *The Sage in Israel and the Ancient Near East*. Edited by J. G. Gammie and L. G. Perdue. Winona Lake, Ind.: Eisenbrauns, 1990.

> Applies a sociocultural approach to explain the "canonical memory" of Solomon, which incorporates diverse material. Focuses on the "Solomonic enterprise," that is, the "large cultural movement" of which Solomon was a part "and not simply the person of the king." In this respect, "Solomon is not simply a historical person, but something of a sociocultural mutation in Israel" (p. 120).

83 C. Fontaine. "The Sage in Family and Tribe." Pp. 155–64 in *The Sage in Israel and the Ancient Near East*. Edited by J. G. Gammie and L. G. Perdue. Winona Lake, Ind.: Eisenbrauns, 1990.

> Reviews the biblical evidence for "the tribe/clan as a logical source for pre-monarchic wisdom traditions" (p. 155), with some attention given to the role of the mother. Suggests that the patterns developed in tribe/clan wisdom "came to influence the later, more formalized roles of the sage in court and school" (p. 164).

84   A. Lemaire. "The Sage in School and Temple." Pp. 165–81 in *The Sage in Israel and the Ancient Near East*. Edited by J. G. Gammie and L. G. Perdue. Winona Lake, Ind.: Eisenbrauns, 1990.

Argues that wisdom texts had their setting in schools (probably in Jerusalem) and were used as the basis for instruction by teachers (the sages). These schools were at first associated with the royal court but became increasingly popularized.

85   C. Westermann. *Roots of Wisdom: The Oldest Proverbs of Israel and Other Peoples*. Translated by J. Daryl Charles. Louisville: Westminster/John Knox, 1995. Original Title: *Wurzeln der Weisheit*. Göttingen: Vandenhoeck und Ruprecht, 1990.

Examines a wide range of wisdom-related topics, arguing that ancient Israelite wisdom had agrarian roots and developed to accommodate Israel's later urban setting. Focuses mainly on Proverbs.

86   R. N. Whybray. "The Sage in the Israelite Royal Court." Pp. 133–39 in *The Sage in Israel and the Ancient Near East*. Edited by J. G. Gammie and L. G. Perdue. Winona Lake, Ind.: Eisenbrauns, 1990.

Overview of the political functions of Israelite wisdom including the wisdom of David and Solomon, royal courtiers, and the court as an intellectual center.

87   E. W. Heaton. *The School Tradition of the Old Testament*. Oxford: Oxford University Press, 1994.

Broad examination of the "weighty and diverse" (p. 1) evidence for the existence of schools in preexilic Israel, which gave rise to and received instruction from biblical wisdom literature. This school tradition was characterized by "the teaching of a moral and reasonable faith, which is detached . . . from national triumphalism" (p. 6).

88   R. E. Murphy. "Israelite Wisdom and the Home." Pp. 199–212 in *Où demeures-tu? (Jn 1,38): La maison depuis monde biblique* [FS G. Couturier]. Edited by J. C. Petit. Saint-Laurent, Quebec: Fides, 1994.

Original life-setting of wisdom is to be found in the home rather than the school.

89   M. Sneed. "Wisdom and Class: A Review and Critique." *JAAR* 62 (1994): 651–72.

Previous attempts at locating biblical wisdom in a particular social class have failed to define class clearly and have assumed that individuals within classes behave consistently. Includes survey of scholarship and problems inherent in defining class.

90 S. Weeks. *Early Israelite Wisdom*. Oxford: Clarendon, 1994. Reexamination of the popular hypothesis that biblical wisdom originated in the education of court administrators by paying especial attention to the non-Israelite literature.

1.5. Theology

Until relatively recently, modern treatments of OT theology have tended to give weighted attention to the Pentateuch, historical books, and the prophetic corpus, that is, Heilsgeschichte. Typically, wisdom theology has either been slighted or made to conform to theological categories better suited to other genres. For roughly the past twenty to thirty years, however, more attention has been given not only to the theological content of the wisdom literature in its own right, but to the place of wisdom theology in the spectrum of the diverse theological perspectives of the OT as a whole.

1.5.1. General

91 W. Zimmerli. "Concerning the Structure of Old Testament Wisdom." Translated by B. W. Kovacs. Pp. 175–207 in *Studies in Ancient Israelite Wisdom*. Edited by J. L. Crenshaw. New York: KTAV, 1976. Original title: "Zur Struktur der alttestamentlichen Weisheit." *ZAW* 10, no. 3 (1933): 177–204.
Attempts to answer whether the essence of wisdom "grows up out of a knowledge and recognition of a fixed, binding obligation," that is, a response to divine order, or whether "it is a question which originates with the individual person, ultimately being oriented around him alone" (p. 178). The author answers that "man's requirements in life are best cared for within the divine order of the world" (p. 198).

92 W. Harrelson. "Wisdom and Pastoral Theology." *Andover Newton Quarterly* 7 (1966): 3–11.
Popular presentation of the value of OT wisdom (particularly Job and Ecclesiastes) for the religious life. Wisdom holds in tension the polarity of the sacred and the profane. "[F]eatures of man's world are knowable on the basis of a critical assessment of man's actual daily experience" (p. 8).

93 B. Gemser. "The Spiritual Structure of Biblical Aphoristic Wisdom: A Review of Recent Standpoints and Theories." Pp. 138–49 in *Adhuc Loquitur: Collected Essays of Dr. B. Gemser*. Edited by A. Van Selms and A. S. Van der Woude. Leiden: E. J. Brill, 1968. Reprinted in J. L. Crenshaw's *Studies in Ancient Israelite Wisdom*. New York: KTAV, 1976, pp. 208–19.

Discusses two issues raised by W. Zimmerli's (#91) understanding of the structure of wisdom and subsequent scholarly reaction: the anthropocentrism of wisdom and the non-authoritative nature of wisdom as "advice."

94 R. E. Murphy. "The Hebrew Sage and Openness to the World." Pp. 219–44 in *Christian Action and Openness to the World* (Villanova University Symposium II, III). Villanova, Pa.: Villanova University Press, 1970.

Defines "openness" to the world as "an attitude begotten of *reflection* upon the wide gamut of human experience, and a *discernment* of values therein" (p. 219). Such an attitude was maintained by the sages "because all things were good, created by the Lord, and man himself had received the commission to rule the earth" (p. 239).

95 J. L. Crenshaw. "In Search of Divine Presence: Some Remarks Preliminary to a Theology of Wisdom." *Review and Expositor* 74 (1977): 353–69.

Overview of the study of the theology of wisdom. Israel's wisdom tradition is diverse. The theological link between wisdom in ancient Israel and its significance for today can be found "in a search for divine presence" (p. 366).

96 H.-J. Hermission. "Observation on the Creation Theology in Wisdom." Pp. 43–57 in *Israelite Wisdom: Theological and Literary Essays in Honor of Samuel Terrien*. Edited by J. G. Gammie et al. Missoula: Scholars, 1978.

Following the work of W. Zimmerli (#91), the author seeks to establish the generally accepted view that wisdom theology is creation theology. Creation is the continual work of Yahweh in establishing a well-ordered world.

97 R. E. Murphy. "Wisdom—Theses and Hypotheses." Pp. 35–42 in *Israelite Wisdom: Theological and Literary Essays in Honor of Samuel Terrien*. Edited by J. G. Gammie et al. Missoula: Scholars, 1978.

Biblical wisdom seeks order in human life; is closely tied to creation theology; has both popular and royal roots; cannot be understood in terms of a sacred/secular dichotomy.

98 G. T. Sheppard. *Wisdom as a Hermeneutical Construct: A Study in the Sapientializing of the Old Testament.* BZAW, 151. Berlin/New York: Walter de Gruyter, 1980.

Three case studies (Sir. 24:3–29; 16–24–17:14; Bar. 3:9–4:4) provide insight into the "theological function of wisdom in the exilic and post-exilic periods" (p. 1). Wisdom became central for interpreting Torah and the Prophets.

99 J. L. Crenshaw. "Wisdom and Authority: Sapiential Rhetoric and Its Warrants." Pp. 10–29 in *Congress Volume: Vienna, 1980.* VTSup 32. Leiden: E. J. Brill, 1981.

Sages spoke with divine authority, yet "self-consciously endeavor[ed] to master the art of suasion at the same time" (pp. 10–11). Focuses on Job but with implications for other wisdom texts.

100 R. B. Zuck. "A Theology of the Wisdom Books and Song of Songs." Pp. 207–55 in *A Biblical Theology of the Old Testament.* Edited by R. B. Zuck. Chicago: Moody, 1991.

General theological observations on the nature of wisdom. Specific nature of wisdom in Job, Proverbs, Ecclesiastes, and Song of Songs.

101 R. E. Clements. *Wisdom in Theology.* Carlisle: Paternoster/Grand Rapids: Eerdmans, 1992.

Introductory chapter discusses basic issues of ANE background, the development of Israelite wisdom literature, and wisdom as foundation for theology. Following chapters consider wisdom and the world, health, politics, the household, and the divine realm. Provided basis for late Israelite noncultic, universalistic worldview.

102 J. Barr. "Divine Action and Hebrew Wisdom." Pp. 1–12 in *The Making and Remaking of Christian Doctrine: Essays in Honour of Maurice Wiles.* Edited by S. Coakley and D. A. Pailin. Oxford: Clarendon, 1993.

"In the Wisdom literature God seems not to act, or to act only little and in a muted or distant way" (p. 6). Includes discussions on divine retribution and creation.

103 J. L. Crenshaw. "The Concept of God in Old Testament Wisdom." Pp. 1–18 in *In Search of Wisdom: Essays in Memory of*

John. G. Gammie. Edited by L. G. Perdue et al. Louisville: Westminster/John Knox, 1993.

Concepts of justice and mercy; universalism and particularism.

104 L. G. Perdue. *Wisdom and Creation: The Theology of Wisdom Literature.* Nashville: Abingdon, 1994.

A broad yet detailed investigation of the theology of wisdom literature. Argues that the sages interacted to a large extent with the theology of creation, and takes as the point of departure the creation metaphors employed by the sages, particularly cosmology and anthropology. Includes an overview of various issues involved in and approaches to the theology of wisdom, as well as specific discussions of the theology of Proverbs, Job, Qoheleth, Ben Sira, and Wisdom of Solomon.

1.5.2. Wisdom vis-à-vis OT Theology

105 R. H. Pfeiffer. "Wisdom and Vision in the Old Testament." *ZAW* 52 (1943): 93–102. Reprinted in J. L. Crenshaw's *Studies in Ancient Israelite Wisdom.* New York: KTAV, 1976, pp. 305–13.

Attributes to wisdom a significant role, along with prophecy, in "the religious progress of Israel" by providing the "intellectual content" to Israel's newfound "universal scope and religious character" (p. 93).

106 J. C. Rylaarsdam. *Revelation in Jewish Wisdom Literature.* Chicago: University of Chicago Press, 1946.

Classic study of the tension in biblical and postbiblical wisdom literature between human reason and divine revelation. Both of these elements "oppose each other but are held in tension by the awareness that they both rest on a common foundation" (p. x). Particular mention is made of the role of revelation and authority in the Christian life.

107 J. F. Priest. "Where Is Wisdom to Be Placed?" *JAAR* 31 (1963): 275–82. Reprinted in J. L. Crenshaw's *Studies in Ancient Israelite Wisdom.* New York: KTAV, 1976, pp. 281–88.

Argues for the relevance of wisdom in OT theology by seeing wisdom as reflections on creation as the medium for revelation.

108 W. Zimmerli. "The Place and Limit of Wisdom in the Framework of the Old Testament Theology." *Scottish Journal of Theol-*

ogy 17 (1964): 146–58. Reprinted in J. L. Crenshaw's *Studies in Ancient Israelite Wisdom*. New York: KTAV, 1976, pp. 314–26. Wisdom can only be properly understood within the framework of a theology of creation. Wisdom theology highlights the creator God, "who joined Himself to His people by His encounter with them in history" (p. 158).

109 J. L. McKenzie. "Reflections on Wisdom." *JBL* 86 (1967): 1–9. Personal reflections on the importance of understanding and appreciating Israel's wisdom tradition. Wisdom's approach to reality is the "conviction of the validity of experience" (p. 8).

110 W. Brueggemann. *In Man We Trust: The Neglected Side of Biblical Faith*. Atlanta: John Knox, 1972. Reexamination of biblical theology in light of often neglected wisdom literature, "those traditions which affirm the world, celebrate culture, and affirm human responsibility and capability" (p. 7).

111 R. E. Murphy. "Wisdom and Yahwism." Pp. 117–126 in *No Famine in the Land* (FS J. L. McKenzie). Missoula: Scholars, 1975. Argues against the somewhat popular scholarly view that wisdom is incompatible with Israelite faith. Examines three crucial assumptions that perpetuate such a dichotomy.

112 J. J. Collins. "The Biblical Precedent for Natural Theology." *JAAR* 45, no. 1, Suppl. B (1977): 35–67. The wisdom tradition is relevant for biblical theology for four reasons: it is an integral part of biblical tradition; it treats the religious dimension of human experience; it attempts to engage biblical traditions; "natural theology" is not restricted to the wisdom literature.

113 J. L. Crenshaw. *A Whirlpool of Torment: Israelite Traditions of God as an Oppressive Presence*. Philadelphia: Fortress, 1984. That God's presence in the OT was often seen negatively is supported by Genesis 22, Job, Ecclesiastes, the confessions of Jeremiah, and Psalm 73. Pain, doubt, testing, and suffering are common biblical phenomena and do not fit easily in a covenantal-credal model of OT theology.

114 R. E. Murphy. "Religious Dimensions of Israelite Wisdom." Pp. 449–58 in *Ancient Israelite Religion: Essays in Honor of Frank Moore Cross*. Edited by P. D. Miller Jr. et al. Philadelphia: Fortress, 1987.

Isolates one religious dimension, the fear of God, to show that "[a]lthough wisdom seems to be taken up with ordinary, everyday events, it retains its basic relationship to God, and the fear of the Lord is an essential ingredient in this achievement" (p. 456).

115 R. E. Clements. "Wisdom." Pp. 67–83 in *It Is Written: Scripture Citing Scripture.* Edited by D. A. Carson and H. G. M. Williamson. Cambridge: Cambridge University Press, 1988.

Discussion of three areas where "wisdom developed a direct and positive interest in the emergent biblical tradition at a surprisingly early stage" (p. 68): creation and its mythology, the concept of *tôrâ*, and Solomon's role in the inception of Israel's wisdom tradition.

116 R. E. Murphy. "Wisdom Literature and Biblical Theology." *BTB* 24 (1994): 4–7.

Wisdom literature has rich theological potential. Concentrates on the female element in wisdom as a biblical balance to patriarchalism.

1.5.3. Theodicy

117 R. J. Williams. "Theodicy in the Ancient Near East." *Canadian Journal of Theology* 2 (1956) 14–26. Reprinted in *Theodicy in the Old Testament.* Edited by J. L. Crenshaw. Philadelphia: Fortress, 1983, pp. 42–56.

Theodicy in the OT compared to ANE.

118 J. L. Crenshaw. "Popular Questioning of the Justice of God in Ancient Israel." *ZAW* 82 (1970): 380–95. Reprinted in J. L. Crenshaw's *Studies in Ancient Israelite Wisdom.* New York: KTAV, 1976, pp. 289–304.

Argues that the essential question of theodicy is anthropocentric. It concerns not reconciling "the existence of God with the presence of evil," but forging a meaning of existence "in the face of the tentacles of death" (p. 382). The point of departure for the discussion is not God but the human condition.

119 B. L. Mack. "Wisdom Myth and Mythology." *Int* 24 (1970): 46–60.

The exile drove the wisdom tradition to deal with the problem of theodicy in creative ways, namely, employing Egyptian wisdom mythology, that affirmed Yahweh's lordship over creation.

120 J. L. Crenshaw (ed.). *Theodicy in the Old Testament*. Philadelphia: Fortress, 1983.

> Collection of eight essays (dated from 1905–75) from various scholars (including Eichrodt, von Rad, Buber, Crenshaw) on the theodicy issue in the OT. Includes essays on the wisdom books as well as Psalm 73, Jeremiah, Ben Sira, and the ANE.

1.5.4. Skepticism

121 J. F. Priest. "Humanism, Skepticism, and Pessimism in Israel." *JAAR* 36 (1968): 311–26.

> Humanism ("man's capacity to confront human life and cope with its problems" [p. 313]) describes Israel's wisdom tradition. Results in skepticism, which is itself impossible without religion. Religion, however, is also impossible without skepticism.

122 R. Davidson. "Some Aspects of the Theological Significance of Doubt in the Old Testament." *Annual of the Swedish Theological Institute* 7 (1968–69): 41–52.

> Doubt, as seen particularly in Job and Ecclesiastes, has positive theological significance in OT theology. Also discusses doubt in the Psalms and Prophets.

123 J. L. Crenshaw. "The Human Dilemma and Literature of Dissent." Pp. 235–58 in *Tradition and Theology in the Old Testament*. Edited by D. A. Knight. Philadelphia: Fortress, 1977.

> Dissent, or protest, is characteristic of the OT, and receives its most forceful expression in Job and Ecclesiastes. OT "baptizes" skepticism and juxtaposes it to faith, holding neither as primary.

124 S. Terrien. "The Play of Wisdom." Pp. 350–89 in *The Elusive Presence: Toward a New Biblical Theology*. Religious Perspectives, 26. San Francisco: Harper & Row, 1978.

> Treatment of the theology of various issues of wisdom literature: personification of wisdom (Job and Proverbs), "A Masque of Revolt" (skepticism), and "Modest Doubt" (Qoheleth).

125 J. L. Crenshaw. "The Birth of Skepticism in Ancient Israel." Pp. 1–19 in *The Divine Helmsman: Studies on God's Control of Human Events, Presented to Lou H. Silberman*. Edited by J. L. Crenshaw and S. Sandmel. New York: KTAV, 1980.

> Skepticism in Israel's wisdom tradition "denied God's goodness if not his very existence," and "portrayed men and

women as powerless to acquire essential truth" (p. 15). These
sages "refused to take confessional statements concerning
divine control of human events at face value, and they insisted
that boasts about human ingenuity also be taken *cum grano
salis*" (p. 15).

1.6. Wisdom Influence outside Wisdom Literature

As wisdom literature came to command more scholarly interest,
studies began to emerge that explored the far-reaching influence of
wisdom in the OT outside the wisdom corpus itself. Although some
studies caution (rightly so) against a trendy "pan-wisdom" approach
(see #126), it is safe to say that wisdom should not be restricted to
those specific books called "wisdom literature," a designation which
is itself not only of modern invention but of somewhat diverse content. Characteristics of wisdom can be found throughout the major
genres of the OT.

1.6.1. General

126 J. L. Crenshaw. "Method in Determining Wisdom Influence upon
'Historical Literature.'" *JBL* 88 (1969): 129–42. Reprinted in J. L.
Crenshaw's *Studies in Ancient Israelite Wisdom*. New York:
KTAV, 1976, pp. 481–94.
     Argues against the popular trend at the time to exaggerate the
     degree to which wisdom influence is detectable in nonsapi-
     ential literature. Refers specifically to the Joseph narrative
     (contra von Rad [128]), the succession narrative (contra Why-
     bray, *The Succession Narrative*) and Esther (contra Talmon
     [#137]).

127 D. F. Morgan. *Wisdom in the Old Testament Traditions*. Atlanta:
John Knox/Oxford: Blackwell, 1981.
     Chronological investigation of wisdom teachings and other
     wisdom elements in the non-wisdom books of the OT in an
     effort to show the pervasive influence of wisdom in the OT.

1.6.2. Pentateuch

128 L. Alonso Schökel. "Sapiential and Covenant Themes in Genesis 2–3." *Theology Digest* 13 (1965): 3–10. Reprinted in J. L. Crenshaw's *Studies in Ancient Israelite Wisdom*. New York: KTAV,
1976, pp. 468–80.

Discusses among other things sapiential elements in the Fall narrative. Includes "knowledge" and "shrewdness."

129 G. von Rad. "The Joseph Narrative and Ancient Wisdom." Pp. 292–300 in *The Problem of the Hexateuch and Other Essays.* Translated by E. W. Trueman Dicken. Edinburgh/London: Oliver & Boyd, 1966. Original Title: *Gesammelte Studien zum Alten Testament.* München: C. Kaiser, 1958/73. Reprinted in J. L. Crenshaw's *Studies in Ancient Israelite Wisdom.* New York: KTAV, 1976, pp. 439–47.

The Joseph story exhibits features of Egyptian wisdom, particularly regarding education and theology.

130 G. W. Coats. "The Joseph Story and Ancient Wisdom: A Reappraisal." *CBQ* 35 (1973): 285–97.

Arguing against von Rad's seminal article (#128) and following Crenshaw's critique of von Rad (#126), the author concludes on the basis of the genre and setting of the Joseph narrative that it is not a wisdom novella, although it exhibits some wisdom elements.

131 M. Weinfeld. "The Origin of Humanism in Deuteronomy." *JBL* 80 (1967): 241–47.

The source of the humanism in the Deuteronomic law code is not the legal or prophetic traditions, but wisdom, particularly Proverbs.

132 M. Weinfeld. *Deuteronomy and the Deuteronomistic School.* Oxford: Oxford University Press, 1972.

The Deuteronomistic literature is a creation of scribal circles of the Jerusalem court around the time of Josiah and thereafter. In particular, influence of wisdom in the Deuteronomistic composition is seen, for example, in parallels between the two, fear of God, humanism, didacticism, doctrine of reward (i.e., theodicy).

133 C. Brekelmans. "Wisdom Influence in Deuteronomy." Pp. 28–38 in *La Sagesse de l'Ancien Testament.* Edited by M. Gilbert. BETL, 51. Leuven: Leuven University Press, 1979.

Strengths and weaknesses of Weinfeld's thesis (#1323). Concludes that, although Weinfeld's work is of considerable value, more work can be done particularly concerning methodology in discerning wisdom influence.

134 J. R. Boston. "The Wisdom Influence upon the Song of Moses." *JBL* 87 (1968): 198–202.

Analysis of Deuteronomy 32:1–43 supports Weinfeld's thesis that wisdom's provenance is to be found in the court scribes of Hezekiah and Josiah. (See M. Weinfeld, "Deuteronomy—The Present State of Inquiry," *JBL* 86 [1967]: 249–62. See also #133.)

135   B. S. Childs. "The Birth of Moses." *JBL* 84 (1965): 109–22.
In addition to being an example of the common ANE "exposure saga," Moses' birth narrative is also an historicized wisdom tale, which bears close resemblance to the Joseph narrative. Wisdom elements in the Moses narrative are: relative absence of God's role; Pharaoh as a "wicked fool"; personal piety; positive view of the Egyptian princess.

136   T. Frymer-Kensky. "The Sage in the Pentateuch: Soundings." Pp. 275–87 in *The Sage in Israel and the Ancient Near East*. Edited by J. G. Gammie and L. G. Perdue. Winona Lake, Ind.: Eisenbrauns, 1990.
Wisdom elements in the Pentateuch include women's roles in influencing the course of human events, Joseph (who is called a "sage"), the "intellectual" language of Deuteronomy, the emphasis on experience in Exodus, specialized knowledge in Leviticus.

1.6.3. Historical Books

137   S. Talmon. "'Wisdom' in the Book of Esther." *VT* 13 (1963): 419–55.
The book of Esther is an attempt to "present a generalizing wisdom-tale and traditional wisdom-motifs in a specific historical setting" (p. 453). Esther is a "historicized wisdom-tale . . . an enactment of standard 'Wisdom' motifs which are present in other biblical narratives" (p. 426).

138   J. Blenkinsopp. "The Sage, the Scribe, and Scribalism in the Chronicler's Work." Pp. 307–15 in *The Sage in Israel and the Ancient Near East*. Edited by J. G. Gammie and L. G. Perdue. Winona Lake, Ind.: Eisenbrauns, 1990.
Including Chronicles with Ezra–Nehemiah, argues for the presence of wisdom elements in this corpus. Scribes acted as royal officials, writers, recorders, and notaries. They were also involved in the instruction of Torah (particularly Ezra), which eventually led to the identification of wisdom and Torah (apart from priesthood) in later Judaism (Ben Sira).

139 P. K. McCarter Jr. "The Sage in the Deuteronomistic History." Pp. 289–93 in *The Sage in Israel and the Ancient Near East.* Edited by J. G. Gammie and L. G. Perdue. Winona Lake, Ind.: Eisenbrauns, 1990.

Solomon's partial realization of the wisdom ideal, particularly in the older literary sources, is transformed by the late compilers of the material in equating wisdom with the study of Torah and the godly life.

140 J. Blenkinsopp. "Wisdom in the Chronicler's Work." Pp. 19–30 in *In Search of Wisdom: Essays in Memory of John. G. Gammie.* Edited by L. G. Perdue et al. Louisville: Westminster/John Knox, 1993.

The author of Chronicles and Ezra–Nehemiah, likely a Levite, employed the literary medium of "edifying history," and in this sense may be regarded as sapiential.

1.6.4. Prophets
1.6.4.1 General

141 J. Lindblom. "Wisdom in the Old Testament Prophets." Pp. 192–204 in *Wisdom in Israel and in the Ancient Near East: Presented to Professor Harold Henry Rowley.* Edited by M. Noth and D. W. Thomas. VTSup 3. Leiden: E. J. Brill, 1955.

Prophets were well acquainted with wisdom, and their works show its influence on them. They were "cognizant of the existence of 'wise men' as a definite class in Israel" (p. 204).

142 W. McKane. *Prophets and Wise Men.* Studies in Biblical Theology, 44. London: SCM/Naperville, Ill.: Allenson, 1965.

Exploration of the tension and incompatibility between prophet and statesman in the OT. Focuses largely on the prophetic use of wisdom vocabulary to attack "old wisdom."

143 D. F. Morgan. "Wisdom and the Prophets." Pp. 209–44 in *Studia Biblica 1978 I: Papers on Old Testament and Related Themes.* Edited by E. A. Livingstone. Sixth International Congress on Biblical Studies. JSOTSup 11. Sheffield: JSOT, 1979.

Prophets show wisdom influence in two ways: (1) borrowing from identifiable wisdom literature; (2) less direct contact with the wisdom tradition.

144 R. C. Van Leeuwen. "The Sage in the Prophetic Literature." Pp. 295–306 in *The Sage in Israel and the Ancient Near East.* Edited by J. G. Gammie and L. G. Perdue. Winona Lake, Ind.: Eisenbrauns, 1990.

Sages are responsible for the redaction of the prophetic books. As actual figures, however, they typically act as opponents of the prophets. As such, these sages transgress the bounds of human wisdom by defying God's messengers.

1.6.4.2. Isaiah

145 J. Fichtner. "Isaiah among the Wise." Translated by B. W. Kovacs. Pp. 429–38 in *Studies in Ancient Israelite Wisdom*. Edited by J. L. Crenshaw. New York: KTAV, 1976. Original Title: "Jesaja unter den Weisen." *Theologische Literaturzeitung* 74 (1949): 75–80. Reprinted in K. D. Fricke's *Gottes Weisheit: Gesamelte Studien zum Alten Testament* (J. Fichtner Festschrift). Stuttgart: Calver, 1965, pp. 18–26.

> In view of the fact that wisdom is not simply a postexilic phenomenon, the author looks at the relationship between the prophet Isaiah and wisdom. Isaiah is at the same time an opponent and disciple of wisdom.

146 J. W. Whedbee. *Isaiah and Wisdom*. Nashville: Abingdon, 1971.

> Argues for Isaiah's indebtedness to Israel's wisdom traditions. Builds on J. Fichtner's seminal essay (#145). Wisdom elements in Isaiah include the use of parables and proverbs, woe speeches, and the term "counsel" (*ʿēṣâ*).

147 J. Jensen. *The Use of* tôrâ *by Isaiah: His Debate with the Wisdom Tradition*. CBQMS, 3. Washington, D.C.: Catholic Biblical Association, 1973.

> Rather than reflecting priestly, prophetic, or legal terminology, "Isaiah's use of the term *tôrâ* reflects wisdom usage ('wise instruction')" (p. 1), specifically, his polemic against "the wise." Builds on J. Fichtner's work (#145), as well as the works of Whedbee (#146), McKane (#142), and von Rad (#18 and *Old Testament Theology*).

148 J. M. Ward. "The Servant's Knowledge in Isaiah 40–55." Pp. 121–36 in *Israelite Wisdom: Theological and Literary Essays in Honor of Samuel Terrien*. Edited by J. G. Gammie et al. Missoula: Scholars, 1978.

> This portion of Isaiah "seems to be a response to an intellectual outlook [i.e., skepticism] exhibited most fully in the Book of Job—and later in Ecclesiastes" (p. 122)

1.6.4.3. Other

149 S. Terrien. "Amos and Wisdom." Pp. 108–15 in *Israel's Prophetic Heritage*. Edited by B. W. Anderson and W. Harrelson. New York: Harper & Row, 1962. Reprinted in J. L. Crenshaw's *Studies in Ancient Israelite Wisdom*. New York: KTAV, 1976, pp. 448–55.
Investigates presence of wisdom language, style, and ideas in Amos. Suggests that prophets, priests, and sages were not isolated from each other.

150 J. L. Crenshaw. "The Influence of the Wise upon Amos." *ZAW* 79 (1967): 42–52.
Review and assessment of recent literature on wisdom influence on Amos.

151 D. Gowan. "Habakkuk and Wisdom." *Perspective* 9 (1968): 157–66.
"Habakkuk shows close affinities with the 'skeptical wisdom' of Job, Koheleth, Prov. 30, and some of the Psalms" (p. 158). These affinities are not the result of Habakkuk's association with a closed "wisdom school," but evidence of the pervasiveness of wisdom in "typical Israelite thought" (p. 165).

152 W. Brueggemann. "The Epistemological Crisis of Israel's Two Histories (Jer 9:22–23)." Pp. 85–105 in *Israelite Wisdom: Theological and Literary Essays in Honor of Samuel Terrien*. Edited by J. G. Gammie et al. Missoula: Scholars, 1978.
"Jeremiah spoke out of a complex relation with Israel's sapiential tradition," both resembling its form while condemning its foolish simplicity (p. 99).

153 G. M. Landes. "Jonah: A *Mœßœl* ?" Pp. 137–58 in *Israelite Wisdom: Theological and Literary Essays in Honor of Samuel Terrien*. Edited by J. G. Gammie et al. Missoula: Scholars, 1978.
Building on the work of G. E. Mendenhall (and contra J. Muilenburg and I. Mendelsohn), Landes studies the *māšāl* in the OT and concludes that the book of Jonah on various levels basically conforms to the genre.

154 W. McKane. "Jeremiah 13:12–14: A Problematic Proverb." Pp. 107–20 in *Israelite Wisdom: Theological and Literary Essays in Honor of Samuel Terrien*. Edited by J. G. Gammie et al. Missoula: Scholars, 1978.

Detailed exegesis of this "proverb," focusing mainly on the meaning of *nēbel* (jar or skin) while interacting with the versions and the insights of Rashi and Kimchi.

155 R. C. Van Leeuwen. "Scribal Wisdom and Theodicy in the Book of the Twelve." Pp. 31–49 in *In Search of Wisdom: Essays in Memory of John. G. Gammie.* Edited by L. G. Perdue et al. Louisville: Westminster/John Knox, 1993.

"[T]he end-redaction of the Book of the Twelve is sapiential in character and . . . throughout Hosea–Micah this redaction employs the bipolar attribute formula on YHWH's name from Exod 34:6–7 as a base text in developing an overarching theodicy vis-à-vis the divine judgments of 722 and 587 BCE" (p. 49).

1.7. Wisdom and Apocalyptic

There are similarities between the wisdom and apocalyptic genres. The origins of apocalyptic are at least to some extent (by no means exclusively) to be found in wisdom thinking.

156 J. G. Gammie. "Spatial and Ethical Dualism in Jewish Wisdom and Apocalyptic Literature." *JBL* 93 (1974): 356–85.

Attempts to bring clarity to discussions over dualism in apocalyptic, and to show that dualism was as prominent in wisdom as in apocalyptic.

157 B. Otzen. "O.T. Wisdom Literature and Dualistic Thinking in Late Judaism." Pp. 146–57 in *Congress Volume: Edinburgh, 1974.* VTSup 28. Leiden: E. J. Brill, 1974.

Dualistic thinking in intertestamental Judaism is not limited to the cosmic/eschatological sphere of apocalyptic, but to the psychological/ethical sphere. This ethical dualism can be traced back to OT wisdom literature. Builds on von Rad's understanding of apocalyptical dualism stemming from biblical wisdom (#18).

158 J. Z. Smith. "Wisdom and Apocalyptic." Pp. 131–56 in *Religious Syncretism in Antiquity: Essays in Conversation with Geo Widengren.* Edited by B. A. Pearson. Missoula: Scholars, 1975. Reprinted in P. D. Hanson's *Visionaries and Their Apocalypses.* Issues in Religion and Theology, 2. Philadelphia: Fortress /London: SCM, 1983, pp. 100–120.

Explores extrabiblical material to determine the relationship between biblical wisdom and apocalyptic. Both are scribal phenomena, engaged in problem solving and *Listenwissenschaft.* Wisdom, however, is located in the court, whereas apocalyptic is a response to the cessation of native kingship.

159 S. J. De Vries. "Observations on Quantitative and Qualitative Time in Wisdom and Apocalyptic." Pp. 263–76 in *Israelite Wisdom: Theological and Literary Essays in Honor of Samuel Terrien.* Edited by J. G. Gammie et al. Missoula: Scholars, 1978.

Wisdom and apocalyptic "share an essential ideological kinship in their conception of time and history," which also serves to isolate these movements within the "mainstream of Israel's religious literature" (p. 263).

160 J. G. Gammie. "From Prudentialism to Apocalypticism: The Houses of the Sages amid the Varying Forms of Wisdom." Pp. 479–97 in *The Sage in Israel and the Ancient Near East.* Edited by J. G. Gammie and L. G. Perdue. Winona Lake, Ind.: Eisenbrauns, 1990.

Discusses shifting notions of wisdom in family, king, and nation over time. Major paradigm shifts were brought about by (1) the introduction of the notion of the afterlife ("eschatologizing of wisdom") and (2) the increased sense of national self-identity vis-à-vis law ("'torahization' of wisdom").

161 J. J. Collins. "Wisdom, Apocalypticism, and Generic Compatibility." Pp. 165–85 in *In Search of Wisdom: Essays in Memory of John G. Gammie.* Edited by L. G. Perdue et al. Louisville: Westminster/John Knox, 1993.

The genre of wisdom was "polymorphous" during the Second Temple period and was adapted for both "this worldly" and apocalyptic worldviews. As such, there is no justification in drawing a sharp distinction between wisdom and apocalypticism, especially as has been done in scholarship concerning teachings attributed to Jesus.

1.8. Wisdom and the Feminine

Recent scholarship has begun focusing more attention on the feminine aspect of wisdom, due in part to the recognition that personified wisdom in the OT, the ANE, and the Second Temple period is a female figure.

162 C. V. Camp. "The Wise Women of 2 Samuel: A Role Model for Women in Early Israel." *CBQ* 43 (1981): 14–29.

"[T]he wise women of Tekoa and Abel, portrayed in 2 Samuel 14 and 20 respectively, are representatives of at least one significant, political role available to women in the years preceding the establishment of the kingship in Israel" (p. 14). This role was rooted in tribal ethos, the origins of which are in "old wisdom."

163 C. V. Camp. "The Female Sage in Ancient Israel and in the Biblical Wisdom Literature." Pp. 185–203 in *The Sage in Israel and the Ancient Near East*. Edited by J. G. Gammie and L. G. Perdue. Winona Lake, Ind.: Eisenbrauns, 1990.

Review of the evidence for the female wisdom element in 2 Samuel 14 and 20, Proverbs, Ben Sira, and the Wisdom of Solomon. Argues that the subsequent "centralization of power and formalization of roles" virtually eliminated the influence of women, its only memory remaining in "the idealized figure of Woman Wisdom" (p. 203).

164 R. Harris. "The Female 'Sage' in Mesopotamian Literature (with an Appendix on Egypt)." Pp. 3–17 in *The Sage in Israel and the Ancient Near East*. Edited by J. G. Gammie and L. G. Perdue. Winona Lake, Ind.: Eisenbrauns, 1990.

The author sets out to infer from the "silence" of the Mesopotamian sources regarding women the varied "wisdom" roles women played in Mesopotamian society, including bureaucrat, poetess, scholar, artist, healer, mantic, and counselor. This reticence is a deliberate "curtailing [of] female influence and authority" by the "traditional patriarchal culture" [p. 3].

165 A. Brenner. "Some Observations on the Figurations of Women in Wisdom Literature." Pp. 192–208 in *Of Prophets' Visions and the Wisdom of the Sages: Essays in Honour of R. Norman Whybray on his Seventieth Birthday*. Edited by H. A. McKay and D. J. A. Clines. JSOTSup 162. Sheffield: JSOT, 1993.

Discusses preoccupation with feminine matters, as seen in rhetorical devices and narrational focalization, in biblical wisdom literature and the Joseph narrative, Esther, and Daniel. Feminine figurations may be "suppressed, misquoted or misread" in masculine biblical discourse (p. 193).

166 J. E. McKinlay. *Gendering Wisdom the Host: Biblical Invitations to Eat and Drink*. JSOTSup 216. Gender, Culture, Theory, 4. Sheffield: Sheffield Academic, 1996.

Feminist interpretation of relevant texts in Proverbs, Ben Sira, and John. Wisdom has suffered a long process of masculinization throughout this period.

1.9. Other

The following essays defy easy categorization, but are of general interest nevertheless. Some of these studies focus on the form and structure of wisdom sayings.

167 R. Gordis. "Quotations in Wisdom Literature." *JQR* 30 (1939–40): 123–47. Reprinted in J. L. Crenshaw's *Studies in Ancient Israelite Wisdom*. New York: KTAV, 1976, pp. 220–44.

An attempt to understand various difficult passages in Ecclesiastes and Job by attributing the unconventional wisdom elements to the writers' use of quotations. Organizes the various types of quotations under appropriate headings.

168 A. R. Johnson. "מָשָׁל." Pp. 162–69 in *Wisdom in Israel and in the Ancient Near East: Presented to Professor Harold Henry Rowley*. Edited by M. Noth and D. W. Thomas. VTSup 3. Leiden: E. J. Brill, 1955.

The root generally implies "likeness," but with several nuances.

169 P. A. H. de Boer. "The Counsellor." Pp. 42–71 in *Wisdom in Israel and in the Ancient Near East: Presented to Professor Harold Henry Rowley*. Edited by M. Noth and D. W. Thomas. VTSup 3. Leiden: E. J. Brill, 1955.

Investigates the function of the counselor in OT wisdom in an effort to shed light on the phenomenon of the personification of wisdom. The counselor is one who knows hidden matters that are important for the future. The role of the counselor is analogous to that of the prophet.

170 L. G. Perdue. *Wisdom and Cult: A Critical Analysis of the Views of Cult in the Wisdom Literatures of Israel and the Ancient Near East*. SBLDS, 30. Missoula: Scholars, 1977.

Discusses view of the cult in Egyptian, Mesopotamian, and Israelite (including psalms) wisdom literature. Concludes that "the traditional wise regarded the realm of the cult to be an important compartment within the orders of reality, and, therefore, merited sapiential scrutiny and demanded sagacious participation" (p. 362).

171 P. J. Nel. " A Proposed Method for Determining the Context of the Wisdom Admonitions." *Journal of Northwest Semitic Languages* 6 (1978): 33–39. (See #482.)

Critical investigation into the biblical wisdom admonitions in their ANE context. Such admonitions in the OT have peculiarities that cannot be fully understood simply on the basis of ANE parallel evidence. Comprehensive method involves ANE setting, function in Israelite religious community, and a careful study of the motivational clauses.

172 J. G. Williams. *Those Who Ponder Proverbs: Aphoristic Thinking and Biblical Literature.* Bible and Literature Series, 2. Sheffield: Almond, 1981.

Far-reaching study that considers aphoristic wisdom within the OT, focusing mainly on Proverbs and Ecclesiastes, as well as Ben Sira, the Synoptic Gospels, and modern literary criticism.

171 J. Blenkinsopp. *Wisdom and Law in the Old Testament: The Ordering of Life in Israel and Early Judaism.* Oxford: Oxford University Press, 1983.

Wisdom and law are "two great rivers which eventually flow together and find their outlet in rabbinic writings and early Christian theology" (p. 130). This tendency is particularly present in Deuteronomy. Wisdom is revelatory and law is the paramount expression of divine wisdom.

174 M. V. Fishbane. "From Scribalism to Rabbinism: Perspectives on the Emergence of Classical Judaism." Pp. 439–56 in *The Sage in Israel and the Ancient Near East.* Edited by J. G. Gammie and L. G. Perdue. Winona Lake, Ind.: Eisenbrauns, 1990.

Review of the emerging identification of wisdom and Torah in the late biblical period, which developed into "Torah piety." Includes discussion of this phenomenon in Daniel, Qumran, and early rabbinic sources.

175 L. G. Perdue. "Cosmology and the Social Order in the Wisdom Tradition." Pp. 457–78 in *The Sage in Israel and the Ancient Near East.* Edited by J. G. Gammie and L. G. Perdue. Winona Lake, Ind.: Eisenbrauns, 1990.

Following sociological theory, the author examines the competing perspectives/paradigms for social organization in Qoheleth and Job, the former representing "order" and the latter "conflict."

176 R. B. Bjornard. "Aging according to the Wisdom Literature." *TBT* 30 (1992): 330–34.

Survey of how the aged are depicted in wisdom literature. Source of stability and tradition in the community.

177 M. V. Fox. "Words for Wisdom." *Zeitschrift für Althebraistik* 6 (1993): 149–69.

Study of the lexical meaning of eight words for wisdom and knowledge. Contains chart of these words in their syntactical environments.

178 T. A. Perry. *Wisdom Literature and the Structure of Proverbs.* University Park: Pennsylvania State University Press, 1993.

Analyzes the various literary structures of wisdom sayings. Includes a glossary of technical terms.

2. Ecclesiastes

Nearly any topic of discussion concerning this most puzzling of biblical books has yielded a broad spectrum of opinions. The primary issue over the past fifty years, as Crenshaw (#186) has observed, has been the inconsistencies within the book itself. Another issue that has generated considerable discussion is the apparent pessimism of Ecclesiastes, especially in the context of the OT canon in general and the wisdom books in particular. Ecclesiastes defies simple categorization, and continues to provide many challenges to the interpreter.

2.1. Anthologies and Introductions

179 M. Jastrow. *A Gentile Cynic: Being a Translation of the Book of Koheleth, Commonly Known as Ecclesiastes, Its Origin, Growth and Interpretation.* New York: Oriole, 1919.
Popularization of critical study on Ecclesiastes. Includes discussion of its origin, growth (i.e., interpolations), and interpretation. Appendix lists passages that are later additions to the book.

180 H. L. Ginsberg. *Studies in Koheleth.* New York, 1950.
Significant discussion of various issues surrounding the book. Most important is the author's development of the hypothesis that Aramaic is the original language of Qoheleth (see also § 2.2.2).

181 H. L. Ginsberg. "Supplementary Studies in Koheleth." *Proceedings of the American Academy for Jewish Research* 21 (1952): 36–62.

Supplements the author's previous study (#180) by revisiting several pericopes. Argues for the essential coherence of the book as opposed to prevailing theories that Qoheleth is a series of disconnected aphorisms.

182 A. F. Rainey. "A Study of Ecclesiastes." *Concordia Theological Monthly* 35 (1964): 148–57.

Overview of introductory issues concerning Ecclesiastes (dialect, provenance, date and authorship, literary character, philosophical concepts).

183 R. Gordis. *Koheleth—The Man and His World: A Study of Ecclesiastes*. Third Edition. New York: Schocken, 1968.

This commentary includes a lengthy introduction (143 pp.), which treats a variety of major scholarly issues concerning Ecclesiastes, and the Hebrew text with translation.

184 S. Breton. "Qoheleth Studies." *BTB* 3 (1973): 22–50.

Survey of recent scholarship to "present briefly the most notable of them and attempt to bring out their distinctive contribution to a better understanding of Qoheleth" (p. 22). Includes discussions on unity, language, origin, style, relationship to traditional wisdom, and *hebel*.

185 S. Breton. "Qohelet: Recent Studies." *Theology Digest* 28 (1980): 147–51.

Review of recent scholorship (commentaries and other studies) to see what progress has been made in our understanding of Ecclesiastes.

186 J. L. Crenshaw. "Qoheleth in Current Research." *HAR* 7 (1983): 41–56.

"[T]he essential issue for more than fifty years [in Qoheleth research] has been the search for an adequate means of explaining inconsistencies within the book" (p. 43). Reviews the four dominant hypotheses: redaction, quotations from traditional wisdom, inconsistencies reflecting life's ambiguities, desire to embrace all of life.

187 R. B. Zuck (ed.). *Reflecting with Solomon: Selected Studies on the Book of Ecclesiastes*. Grand Rapids: Baker, 1994.

Thirty-three previously published essays organized under two headings: overviews of Ecclesiastes and specific themes and passages. Includes bibliography.

2.2. Origins and ANE Influence

The date and language of composition, as well as the specific cultural influences that helped shape Ecclesiastes, are difficult to ascertain with any certainty. The data presented within the book itself are somewhat varied, a fact that has led to the dissemination of a variety of opinions, including Greek, Persian, Phoenician, and Aramaic influences. The view that Ecclesiastes is a postexilic Hebrew composition (albeit with Aramaisims and Mishnaic Hebrew qualities) has achieved some consensus in broader scholarly circles.

2.2.1. ANE Influence

188 H. Ranston. Ecclesiastes and Early Greek Wisdom Literature. London: Epworth, 1925.

Investigates the presence of Greek language or thought in Ecclesiastes by comparing the book to "practical gnomic philosophy" (p. 12) rather than the abstract philosophers. Qoheleth was not well versed in Greek philosophy but drew heavily on Theognis.

189 C. C. Forman. "The Pessimism of Ecclesiastes." JSS 3 (1958): 336–43.

Qoheleth's pessimism is not the result of Greek influence, but places him within the "bounds of Semitic thought" (p. 336).

190 T. Longman III. "Comparative Methods in Old Testament Studies: Ecclesiastes Reconsidered." Theological Students Fellowship Bulletin (March–April 1984): 6–9.

Proper comparison of Ecclesiastes to the literature of the ANE is a most fruitful avenue of research to illuminate the biblical text.

191 J. G. Gammie. "Stoicism and Anti-Stoicism in Qoheleth." HAR 9 (1985): 169–87.

Comparison of Qoheleth and Stoic philosophy. Stoic philosophy had an impact on Qoheleth not only in terms of the content of the book but the form of argumentation. Concerning death, Qoheleth is deliberately anti-Stoic.

192 J. L. Crenshaw. "Youth and Old Age in Qohelet." *HAR* 10 (1986): 1–13.

Contrary to the typically positive evaluation of old age in the ANE as bringing wisdom, Qoheleth presents a gloomy picture of old age. Neither is his evaluation of youth positive. Rather youth is fleeting and even futile.

193 J. L. Kugel. "Qohelet and Money." *CBQ* 51 (1989): 32–49.

A study of the language of several passages having to do with material concerns indicates that Qoheleth is rooted in the Persian world (fifth century).

194 B. W. Jones. "From Gilgamesh to Qoheleth." Pp. 349–79 in *The Bible in the Light of Cuneiform Literature: Scripture in Context III*. Edited by W. W. Hallo et al. Ancient Near Eastern Texts and Studies, 8. Lewiston: Mellon, 1990.

"It is certainly possible that the author of Qoheleth could have been aware of the Gilgamesh story in some form, and I have argued that it is probable that he made use of that tradition, at least in Qoh 9:7–9" (p. 372).

195 S. de Jong. "Qohelet and the Ambitious Spirit of the Ptolemaic Period." *JSOT* 61 (1994): 85–96.

Qoheleth's skepticism regarding the fruit of labor was intended as pragmatic advice to curb aristocratic ambitions in his students.

2.2.2. Original Language

196 F. C. Burkitt. "Is Ecclesiastes a Translation?" *Journal of Theological Studies* 23 (1921–22): 22–26.

Argues for an Aramaic original of Ecclesiastes.

197 F. Zimmermann. "The Aramaic Provenance of Qohelet." *JQR* 36 (1945–46): 17–45.

Detailed defense of the thesis that the Hebrew Qoheleth is a translation of an Aramaic original. See also #219.

198 R. Gordis. "The Original Language of Qohelet." *JQR* 37 (1946–47): 67–84.

Argues against Zimmermann's (#197) theory of an Aramaic original. Qoheleth knew and used Aramaic, which gives the book its Aramaic flavor, but he wrote in Hebrew.

199 C. C. Torrey. "The Question of the Original Language of Qoheleth." *JQR* 39 (1948–49): 151–60.

Assesses and defends F. Zimmermann's (#197) thesis that Aramaic is the original language of Qoheleth.

200 R. Gordis. "The Translation Theory of Qohelet Reexamined." *JQR* 40 (1949–50): 103–16.
Follows the author's previous article (#198) and engages the work of Torrey (#199), who defends the Aramaic original of Qoheleth. Torrey does not convincingly demonstrate the theory of Aramaic provenance.

201 F. Zimmermann. "The Question of Hebrew in Qohelet." *JQR* 40 (1949–50): 79–102.
Examination and rebuttal of R. Gordis's (#198) refutation of Zimmermann's (#197) previous defense of the Aramaic provenance of Qohelet. The inadequacies of Gordis's criticisms in the end wind up supporting Zimmermann's thesis.

202 M. J. Dahood. "Canaanite-Phoenician Influence in Qoheleth." *Bib* 33 (1952): 30–52, 191–221.
First of several studies arguing, on the basis of orthography, morphology, syntax, and vocabulary, for the Phoenician background of Qoheleth. (See also the author's follow-up articles in *CBQ* 14 [1952b]: 227–32; *Bib* 39 [1958]: 302–18; *Bib* 43 [1962]: 349–65; *Bib* 47 [1966]: 264–72.)

203 R. Gordis. "Was Qohelet a Phoenician? Some Observations on Method in Research." *JBL* 74 (1955): 103–14.
Assesses the alleged Phoenician influence on Qoheleth, particularly as put forth by Dahood (#202) on the basis of the "canons of scientific research" (p. 103). Phoenician influence cannot be maintained.

204 R. Gordis. "Qohelet and Qumran—A Study of Style." *Bib* 41 (1960): 395–410.
Despite similarities in Hebrew style between Qumran and Qoheleth, the latter is to be placed "within the framework of authentic Hebrew literature, later than that of the classical Biblical period, and earlier than the full development of Mishnaic Hebrew" (p. 410).

205 G. L. Archer Jr. "The Linguistic Evidence for the Date of Ecclesiastes." *Journal of the Evangelical Theological Society* 12 (1969): 167–81.
"No sound argument for the spuriousness of *Qohelet* as a work of Solomon's can be based upon its grammar, language or

style" (p. 181). Follows Dahood in arguing for Phoenician influence. (See #202.)

206 C. F. Whitley. *Koheleth: His Language and Thought.* BZAW, 148. Berlin and New York: de Gruyter, 1979.

Assessment of the work of Zimmermann (#197) and Dahood (#202) concerning the language of Qoheleth. Proposes date between 152 and 45 B.C. (after Ben Sira, transition period from biblical to Mishnaic Hebrew) for the book's composition. An investigation of the thought of Qoheleth corroborates this view.

207 D. C. Fredericks. *Qohelet's Language: Re-evaluating Its Nature and Date.* Lewiston/Queenston: Mellon, 1988.

Includes overview of the varying scholarly opinions on the linguistic provenance of Qoheleth. Grammatical and lexical comparisons of Qoheleth and the various stages of biblical and postbiblical Hebrew, as well as Aramaisms, Persianisms, and Greek influence. Qoheleth is no later than the exilic period, and possibly preexilic.

208 J. R. Davila. "Qoheleth and Northern Hebrew." *MAARAV* 5–6 (1990): 69–87.

Provides evidence for Qoheleth having been influenced by an ancient dialect of northern Hebrew as opposed to theories of Phoenician or Aramaic influence (#s 180, 197, 199, 202).

209 F. Bianchi. "The Language of Qohelet: A Bibliographical Survey." *ZAW* 105 (1993): 210–23.

Survey and evaluation of previous scholarship on this topic. Both Aramaic and Mishnaic Hebrew influenced the language of Qoheleth.

2.2.3. Linguistic Analysis

210 S. J. Du Plessis. "Aspects of Morphological Peculiarities of the Language of Qoheleth." Pp. 164–80 in *De Fructu Oris Sui: Essays in Honour of Adrianus Van Selms.* Edited by I. H. Eybers, F. C. Fensham, et al. Leiden: E. J. Brill, 1971.

Overview of the language of Qoheleth compared to classical Hebrew. Some points of agreement with Qumran, especially with respect to the pronoun and the confusion of Lamed-He and Lamed-Aleph roots. Aramaic influence especially noticeable with nouns.

211 B. Isaksson. *Studies in the Language of Qoheleth, with Special Emphasis on the Verbal System.* Studia Semitica Upsaliensia, 10. Uppsala: Uppsala University Press, 1987.

Structural-linguistic analysis of the syntax of Qoheleth. Although Qoheleth exhibits certain unique syntactical features, the deviations from standard Hebrew are a function of genre. The language of Qoheleth represents a popular (northern) Hebrew dialect.

212 A. Schoors. *The Preacher Sought to Find Pleasing Words: A Study of the Language of Qoheleth.* Orientalia Lovaniensia Analecta, 41. Leuvan: Peeters, 1992.

A linguistic analysis of Ecclesiastes demonstrates that the verbal forms conform to classical Hebrew usage, but the language is characteristic of later Hebrew. Ecclesiastes also displays Aramaisms.

2.3. Theology/Teaching

The following works include both general overviews of Qoheleth's thought and studies that concentrate on more specific issues, most of which deal to some degree with the tensions between faith and skepticism, that is, pleasure and vanity (*hebel*) within Ecclesiastes. A few remaining studies deal with death and the afterlife.

2.3.1. General

213 W. J. Erdman. *Ecclesiastes: The Book of the Natural Man.* Chicago: The Bible Institute Colportage Association, n.d.

Several brief essays that argue that the content of Ecclesiastes is from the perspective of the "natural man," and hence serves as a "preparation for redemption" in Christ" (p. 9).

214 J. S. Wright. "The Interpretation of Ecclesiastes." *Evangelical Quarterly* 18 (1946): 18–34. Reprinted in R. B. Zuck's *Reflecting with Solomon: Selected Studies on the Book of Ecclesiastes.* Grand Rapids: Baker, 1994, pp. 17–30.

Ecclesiastes is to be interpreted as a united work whose message is ultimately a Christian one: the key to life's meaning is found in Christ.

215 C. W. Reines. "Koheleth on Wisdom and Wealth." *Journal of Jewish Studies* 5 (1954): 80–84.

Qoheleth's statements on wealth suggest that there was a class of wisdom teachers that owned property but that other wisdom teachers were poor and depended on the rich for support.

216 E. Bickerman. "Koheleth (Ecclesiastes) or The Philosophy of an Acquisitive Society." Pp. 139–167 in *Four Strange Books of the Bible*. New York: Schocken, 1967.

Overview of various theological themes, particularly wealth. "[P]leasure is the sole good which acquisitive labor may bring to a money-maker" (p. 158).

217 F. N. Jasper. "Ecclesiastes: A Note for Our Time." *Int* 21 (1967): 259–73.

Ecclesiastes speaks to us today by virtue of its "fundamental honesty" and "sober realism" (p. 272).

218 E. Horton Jr. "Koheleth's Concept of Opposites." *Numen* 19 (1972): 1–21.

Qoheleth offers a "golden mean" between extremes, for example, righteousness and wickedness. This phenomenon is compared to its similar manifestation in Greek philosophy and extrabiblical wisdom literature.

219 F. Zimmermann. *The Inner World of Qohelet*. New York: KTAV, 1973.

Attempts to "provide the student of Qoheleth with an insight into his character and personality in the light of psychological knowledge, and to show how the discordant type of book that he wrote is a mirror of the chain of neuroses that afflicted him; and secondly, to indicate that the language in which he wrote the book was Aramaic and not the Hebrew that we know today" (p. ix).

220 D. A. Hubbard. *Beyond Futility: Messages of Hope from the Book of Ecclesiastes*. Grand Rapids: Eerdmans, 1976.

Thirteen expositions on the teaching of Ecclesiastes. God's simple gifts of work, food, and friends are more profitable than the things people typically lean on to bring meaning to their lives.

221 R. K. Johnston. "'Confessions of a Workaholic': A Reappraisal of Qoheleth." *CBQ* 38 (1976): 14–28.

The purpose of the book is "to pass judgment upon man's misguided endeavors at mastering life by pointing out its limits and mysteries" and to encourage "confidence based in the joy of creation as God's gift" (p. 26).

222 R. N. Whybray. "Qoheleth the Immoralist? (Qoh 7:16–17)." Pp. 191–204 in *Israelite Wisdom: Theological and Literary Essays in Honor of Samuel Terrien*. Edited by J. G. Gammie et al. Missoula: Scholars, 1978.

Discusses "Qoheleth's apparent failure to commend righteous behavior" in Qoheleth 7:16a, which "leaves him open to the charge of teaching immorality" (p. 191). Concludes that the text concerns *self*-righteousness.

223 M. V. Fox. "Qohelet's Epistemology." *HUCA* 58 (1987): 137–55.

"Qohelet's epistemology is essentially (though not consistently) empirical. His procedure is deliberately to seek experience as his primary source of knowledge and to use experiential argumentation in testifying for his claims and validating them" (p. 137). His epistemology is unique in the ANE but not polemical against more typical biblical wisdom.

224 D. A. Garrett. "Qohelet on the Use and Abuse of Political Power." *Trinity Journal* 8 (1987): 159–77.

Examination of eight passages that speak of political power. Qoheleth is a wise and just politician. Neither naive nor corrupt, he works for the good of the nation, biding his time until God's judgment comes.

225 M. V. Fox. *Qohelet and His Contradictions*. JSOTSup 18. Sheffield: Almond, 1989.

The tensions in Qohelet are central to his thought. Several essays lead to three main conclusions: (1) Qoheleth denies the rationality of human existence; (2) he does not attack the mainstream wisdom tradition, but rather expresses disappointment that its ideals are not realized; (3) the search for "inner experience" does not provide meaning in life. Contains brief commentary and paraphrastic translation.

226 J. Ellul. *Reason for Being: A Meditation on Ecclesiastes*. Translated by J. M. Hanks. Grand Rapids: Eerdmans, 1990.

Discussion of a number of themes in Qoheleth organized under three general headings (vanity, wisdom and philosophy, God) that represent the author's synthesis of over fifty years of reflection.

227 E. Levine. "Qohelet's Fool: A Composite Portrait." Pp. 277–94 in *On Humour and the Comic in the Hebrew Bible*. Edited by Y. T. Radday and A. Brenner. Sheffield: JSOT, 1990.

Qoheleth's use of comedy yields a critical, cynical portrayal of the fool as one whose self-perception does not match reality.

228 P. Carny. "Theodicy in the Book of Qohelet." Pp. 71–81 in *Justice and Righteousness: Biblical Themes and Their Influence.* Edited by H. G. Reventlow and Y. Hoffman. Sheffield: JSOT, 1992.

Qohelet's innovative approach to theodicy results from four factors: his picture of God; his denial of just retribution in this life; his denial of retribution in the afterlife; one's inability to justify God.

229 A. R. Ceresko. "Commerce and Calculation: The Strategy of the Book of Qoheleth (Ecclesiastes)." *Indian Theological Studies* 30 (1993): 205–19.

Qoheleth's pessimism regarding commercial society reflects an implicit message of liberation, a message that has not escaped the eye of liberation theologians.

230 M. V. Fox. "Wisdom in Qoheleth." Pp. 115–31 in *In Search of Wisdom: Essays in Memory of J. G. Gammie.* Edited by L. G. Perdue et al. Louisville: Westminster/John Knox, 1993.

For Qoheleth, wisdom "is manifest in three basic aspects: ingenuity, good sense, and intellect" (p. 117). Wisdom fails, however, in accomplishing what it should: it does not provide enough knowledge; it is overwhelmed by "fickle fortune" and death; it is painful. The epilogue acts as a buffer for Qoheleth's words.

2.3.2. Faith/Pleasure versus Skepticism/Vanity

231 M. Kaufmann. "Was Koheleth a Sceptic?" *The Expositor* 9 (1899): 389–400.

Ecclesiastes "presents us with the most pathetic picture of the melancholy side of religion" (p. 399), while at the same time resisting pessimism.

232 C. S. Knopf. "The Optimism of Koheleth." *JBL* 49 (1930): 195–99.

Of the several strands present in Qoheleth, one reveals him as "the champion of a philosophy of hope that flowered above the enervating atmosphere of Hellenistic sophistication" (p. 199).

233 J. Paterson. "The Intimate Journal of an Old-Time Humanist." *Religion in Life* 19 (1950): 245–54.

Qohelet was a bold seeker after truth whose words "[represent] the bankruptcy of human thinking and the barrenness of egoism" (p. 254).

234 F. W. Danker. "The Pessimism of Ecclesiastes." *Concordia Theological Monthly* 22 (1951): 9–32.

  The purpose of pessimism in Ecclesiastes is to highlight the depravity of human existence and that "life is found in the joyful acceptance of the things of this world as God's gifts to be used, but not abused as ends in themselves" (p. 9).

235 L. L. Smith. "A Critical Evaluation of the Book of Ecclesiastes." *Journal of Bible and Religion* 21 (1953): 100–105.

  Ecclesiastes is of little spiritual value. Elevating reason as the sole means of seeking truth, it inspires confusion and cynicism rather than religious devotion.

236 W. E. Staples. "Vanity of Vanities." *Canadian Journal of Theology* 1 (1955): 141–56.

  Examines the popular refrain in Ecclesiastes, which he translates "Mysteries of Mysteries." Qoheleth's many speculations end in his assertion of faith in God and His plan.

237 H. L. Ginsberg. "The Quintessence of Koheleth." Pp. 47–59 in *Biblical and Other Studies*. Edited by A. Altman. Cambridge, Mass.: Harvard University Press, 1963.

  A detailed exegesis of 3:1–4:3 reveals the essence of Qoheleth's teaching: "the only real value a man can get out of life is the utilization of his worldly goods for his enjoyment" (p. 48).

238 J. G. Williams. "What Does It Profit a Man? The Wisdom of Koheleth." *Judaism* 20 (1971): 179–93. Reprinted in J. L. Crenshaw's *Studies in Ancient Israelite Wisdom*. New York: KTAV, 1976, pp. 375–89.

  Ecclesiastes represents Qoheleth's agonizing over "man's inability to move beyond this vaporous existence to a full or satisfying knowledge of the everlasting" (pp. 386–87). Thus, he struggles between the two poles of a retreat from life and intense participation in life's pleasures. Qoheleth's comments, however, do represent a "dim vision of authentic human existence" albeit without an adequate means of expressing that vision (p. 388).

239 J. L. Crenshaw. "The Eternal Gospel (Eccl. 3:11)." Pp. 23–55 in *Essays in Old Testament Ethics*. Edited by J. L. Crenshaw and J. T. Willis. New York: KTAV, 1974.

  Asks whether "man is the object of divine compassion or caprice" (p. 25). Faced with his "inability to discover the true meaning of reality," Qoheleth "shrugged his shoulders and became a lonely man, no longer in dialogue with the world" (p. 48).

240 F. Crüsemann. "The Unchangeable World: The 'Crisis of Wisdom' in Koheleth." Pp. 57–77 in *God of the Lowly: Sociohistorical Interpretations of the Bible*. Edited by W. Schottroff and W. Stegemann. Translated by M. J. O'Connell. N. Y.: Orbis, 1984 Original Title: *Der Gott der kleinen Leute: Sozialgeschichtliche Bibelauslegungen*. München: Chr. Kaiser, 1979.

The theological message of Qoheleth's individualism and cynicism for today's political and social issues.

241 J. T. Walsh. "Despair as a Theological Virtue in the Spirituality of Ecclesiastes." *BTB* 12 (1982): 46–49.

Qoheleth teaches that there must be room in the religious spectrum for those who experience despair, unfairness, and God's silence in life.

242 R. N. Whybray. "Qoheleth, Preacher of Joy?" *JSOT* 23 (1982): 87–98. Reprinted in R. B. Zuck's *Reflecting with Solomon: Selected Studies on the Book of Ecclesiastes*. Grand Rapids: Baker, 1994, pp. 203–12.

Examines seven texts where Qoheleth preaches the pursuit of enjoyment rather than the pessimism evident elsewhere in the book. To enjoy life is to do God's will.

243 A. B. Caneday. "Qoheleth: Enigmatic Pessimist or Godly Sage?" *Grace Theological Journal* (1986): 21–56. Reprinted in R. B. Zuck's *Reflecting with Solomon: Selected Studies on the Book of Ecclesiastes*. Grand Rapids: Baker, 1994, pp. 81–113.

"The enigmatic character and polarized structure of the book of Qoheleth is not a defective quality but rather a deliberate literary device of Hebrew thought patterns designed to reflect the paradoxical and anomalous nature of this present world" (p. 21).

244 N. K. Haden. "Qohelet and the Problem of Alienation." *Christian Scholars Review* 17 (1987): 52–66.

Qoheleth addresses the problems of skepticism and doubt by "teaching that although limitations are inescapable, they do not necessitate a renunciation of meaningful existence" (p. 66). Meaning is elusive but authentic because God exists.

245 R. E. Murphy. "The Faith of Qoheleth." *Word and World* 7 (1987): 253–60.

Qoheleth juxtaposes faith and skepticism—they are not contradictory. For Qoheleth, faith is "the hard but firm acceptance of God on the terms offered to him" (p. 260).

246 G. S. Ogden. "'Vanity' It Certainly Is Not." *The Bible Translator* 38, no. 3 (1987): 301–7.
The term *hebel* should be translated "enigma" or "mystery."

247 P. Kreeft. "Ecclesiastes: Life as Vanity." Pp. 13–58 in Kreeft's *Three Philosophies of Life*. San Francisco: Ignatius, 1989.
Ecclesiastes is a book of life that honestly confronts death.

248 A. Gianto. "The Theme of Enjoyment in Qohelet." *Bib* 73 (1992): 528–32.
"[Joy] is a gift from God that enables humankind to deal with the reality of *hebel* [vanity]" (p. 531).

249 J. E. McKenna. "The Concept of *Hebel* in the Book of Ecclesiastes." *Scottish Journal of Theology* 45 (1992): 19–28.
The meaning of *hebel* cannot be completely encompassed by one English word. It is a category of thought that pervades all of Ecclesiastes and concerns the "contingent rationality" of the world, created by God out of nothing.

250 E. Scheffler. "Qoheleth's Positive Advice." *Old Testament Essays* 6 (1993): 248–71.
Qoheleth is realistically pessimistic, which serves as a call to enjoy life amidst the suffering and absurdity.

251 D. C. Fredericks. *Coping with Transience: Ecclesiastes on Brevity in Life*. Sheffield: JSOT, 1993.
Topical commentary on Ecclesiastes organized around a discussion of *hebel*, which the author translates as "the temporary." Such an understanding of the term helps provide a basis for the book's consistency.

252 M. Kelley. *The Burden of God: Studies in Wisdom and Civilization from the Book of Ecclesiastes*. Minneapolis: Contra Mundum Books, 1993.
"[M]an must relinquish his self-declared independence from God his Creator and Redeemer if he does not want to have lived his life truly in vain" (p. 149).

2.3.3. Death and the Afterlife

253 A. Maltby. "The Book of Ecclesiastes and the After-Life." *Evangelical Quarterly* 35 (1963): 39–44.

"The main object of Ecclesiastes is not to speak of the afterlife, but to show the necessity for it by showing up our earthly vanities for what they are" (p. 44).

254 H. Bream. "Life without Resurrection: Two Perspectives on Qoheleth." Pp. 49–65 in *A Light unto My Path: Old Testament Studies in Honor of Jacob M. Myers*. Edited by H. Bream et al. Gettysburg Theological Studies, 4. Philadelphia: Temple University Press, 1974.

The two perspectives discussed are "Qoheleth's realism with respect to conjecture about the fate of the dead" and his "positive appreciation of this present life" (p. 49). The same points are expressed in the NT, but from the perspective of resurrection faith.

255 M. V. Fox. "Aging and Death in Qohelet 12." *JSOT* 42 (1988): 55–77. Reprinted in R. B. Zuck's *Reflecting with Solomon: Selected Studies on the Book of Ecclesiastes*. Grand Rapids: Baker, 1994, pp. 381–99.

A reading of 12:1–8 and Qoheleth's presentation of aging and death on the literal, symbolic, and figurative levels.

256 B. C. Davis. "Ecclesiastes 12:1–8—Death, an Impetus for Life." *BSac* 148 (1991): 298–317. Reprinted in R. B. Zuck's *Reflecting with Solomon: Selected Studies on the Book of Ecclesiastes*. Grand Rapids: Baker, 1994, pp. 347–66.

Focusing on 12:1–8, the author discusses the meaning of death and dying in Ecclesiastes. Death comes to all, and one must turn to God while there is time in order to meet one's Maker in the afterlife.

257 D. C. Fredericks. "Life's Storms and Structural Unity in Qoheleth 11:1–12:8." *JSOT* 52 (1991): 95–114.

11:7–12:8 should be understood in conjunction with 11:1–6. Such a juxtaposition yields "enjoy life while you can, and such enjoyment should not avoid wise labor" (p. 114).

2.4. Ecclesiastes vis-à-vis *Other Wisdom Books* and the OT

Scholarly energy has focused not only on the tensions within Ecclesiastes itself (see §2.3.2), but between Ecclesiastes and the other wisdom books and the OT as a whole. Opinions differ as to what extent, if at all, the content of Ecclesiastes can be seen as being in essential harmony with the remainder of the biblical canon.

2.4.1. Ecclesiastes and Wisdom

258 R. H. Pfeiffer. "The Peculiar Skepticism of Ecclesiastes." *JBL* 53 (1934): 100–109.

Qoheleth's skepticism shows his general criticism of his Israelite wisdom heritage, particularly its view of God, the world, and humankind. His conclusions show some contact with Greek thought.

259 H. Gese. "The Crisis of Wisdom in Koheleth (1963)." Pp. 141–53 in *Theodicy in the Old Testament*. Edited by J. L. Crenshaw. Philadelphia: Fortress, 1983.

As distinct from earlier Israelite wisdom, for Qoheleth, "the essence of the person is determined not only in that one perceives oneself as an individual but also in that one sets oneself against world affairs as a stranger to the world" (p. 143).

260 G. R. Castellino. "Qohelet and His Wisdom." *CBQ* 30 (1968): 15–28. Reprinted in R. B. Zuck's *Reflecting with Solomon: Selected Studies on the Book of Ecclesiastes*. Grand Rapids: Baker, 1994, pp. 31–43.

Without suppressing the many ambiguities and difficulties in interpreting Qoheleth, it is essentially "in keeping with the spirit of wisdom literature of the OT, although with characteristics of its own" (p. 16).

261 J. A. Loader. "Different Reactions of Job and Qohelet to the Doctrine of Retribution." Pp. 43–48 in *Studies in Wisdom Literature*. Edited by W. C. van Wyk. *Ou-Testamentiese Werkgemeenskap in Suid-Afrika*, 15–16. Potchefstroom: Pro Rege, 1972–73.

While Job proclaims rest for the faithful in the end by turning to God, for Qoheleth, the doctrine of divine retribution does not operate. God is capricious and man's lot in life is helplessness and impotence.

262 R. K. Johnston. "Confessions of a Workaholic: A Reappraisal of Qoheleth." *CBQ* 38 (1976): 14–28. Reprinted in R. B. Zuck's *Reflecting with Solomon: Selected Studies on the Book of Ecclesiastes*. Grand Rapids: Baker, 1994, pp. 133–47.

"Qoheleth need not be considered as standing in resignation on the periphery of the wisdom tradition. Rather, he can be understood as indirectly, but fondly, calling the tradition back to a central focus—the enjoyment of life itself" (pp. 14–15).

263 G. T. Sheppard. "The Epilogue to Qohelet as Theological Commentary." *CBQ* 39 (1977): 182–89.

The epilogue of Ecclesiastes (12:9–14) shares the same perspective as that of Ben Sira and Baruch 3:9–4:4, and provides "a rare glimpse into a comprehensive, canon-conscious formulation of what the purpose of biblical wisdom is" (p. 189).

264 J. L. Crenshaw. "The Shadow of Death in Qoheleth." Pp. 205–16 in *Israelite Wisdom: Theological and Literary Essays in Honor of Samuel Terrien.* Edited by J. G. Gammie et al. Missoula: Scholars, 1978.

Contrary to Proverbs' consistent judgment of death as wholly negative, Qoheleth's view is ambivalent. As such, Qoheleth's view of death is in line with Job and Ben Sira.

265 R. E. Murphy. "Qohelet's 'Quarrel' with the Fathers." Pp. 235–45 in *From Faith to Faith: Essays in Honor of Donald G. Miller on His Seventieth Birthday.* Edited by D. Y. Hadidian. Pittsburgh Theological Monograph Series, 31. Pittsburgh: Pickwick, 1979.

Qoheleth is not in opposition to traditional biblical wisdom. The epilogue, although an editorial addition, gives early justification for reading Qoheleth within the wisdom tradition.

266 R. E. Murphy. "The Sage in Ecclesiastes and Qoheleth the Sage." Pp. 263–71 in *The Sage in Israel and the Ancient Near East.* Edited by J. G. Gammie and L. G. Perdue. Winona Lake, Ind.: Eisenbrauns, 1990.

Brief assessment of Qoheleth's particular contribution to wisdom. "His own wisdom consisted in seeing deeper and further than the traditional wisdom, in purifying it, even to such an extent that it did not appear to be viable. But in style he remained faithful to the tradition of the sages" (p. 271).

267 R. B. Zuck. "God and Man in Ecclesiastes." *BSac* 148 (1991): 46–56. Reprinted in R. B. Zuck's *Reflecting with Solomon: Selected Studies on the Book of Ecclesiastes.* Grand Rapids: Baker, 1994, pp. 213–22.

Examines doctrines of God and man in Ecclesiastes to defend the essential fit of Qoheleth's theology with the rest of wisdom literature.

268 P. P. Chia. "Wisdom, Yahwism, Creation: In Quest of Qoheleth's Theological Thought." *Jian Dao* 3 (1995): 1–32.

As distinct from other wisdom writings, creation theology plays no significant role in Qoheleth's thought.

2.4.2. Ecclesiastes and the OT

269 C. C. Forman. "Koheleth's Use of Genesis." *JSS* 5 (1960): 256–63.
Qoheleth interacted extensively with Genesis 1–11, which constituted his most important source of information on "the nature and destiny of man, the character of human existence, and the fact of God" (p. 263).

270 D. A. Hubbard. "The Wisdom Movement and Israel's Covenant Faith." *TynBul* 17 (1966): 3–33.
There are links between biblical wisdom and the more prevalent notion of covenant in the OT, and these links are not necessarily late by-products of the evolution of the thinking of the sages. Provides several implications for wisdom literature for Christian faith and practice.

271 J. F. Armstrong. "Ecclesiastes in Old Testament Theology." *Princeton Seminary Bulletin* 4 (1983): 16–25.
Ecclesiastes stands as a theological "guardian" that keeps us from an uncritical appropriation of the biblical notion that proper behavior necessarily brings blessing.

272 F. A. Spina. "Qoheleth and the Reformation of Wisdom." Pp. 267–79 in *The Quest for the Kingdom of God.* Edited by H. Huffmon. Winona Lake, Ind.: Eisenbrauns, 1983.
Qoheleth's cynicism should not be understood as secular or humanistic, but as a reaction to the "orthodoxy" of the ritualization of Israelite religion. His thought, rather than being antithetical to "'mainstream' biblical thought" (p. 269), actually reflects more faithfully the Mosaic covenant.

273 A. Schoors. "Koheleth: A Perspective of Life after Death?" *Ephemerides Theologicae Lovanienses* 61 (1985): 295–303.
There is no afterlife for the author of Qoheleth. Death brings complete extinction. Hence, Qoheleth's denial of the afterlife is more pronounced than elsewhere in the OT.

274 W. C. Kaiser Jr. "Integrating Wisdom Theology into Old Testament Theology: Ecclesiastes 3:10–15." Pp. 197–209 in *A Tribute to Gleason Archer: Essays on the Old Testament.* Edited by W. C. Kaiser Jr. and R. F. Youngblood. Chicago: Moody, 1986.

3:10–15 provides the link between wisdom theology and the theology of *tôrâ* and Prophets, namely, through the "fear of Yahweh/God" theme.

275 J. L. Crenshaw. "Ecclesiastes—Odd Book In." *Bible Review* 6 (1990): 28–33.

The force of Qoheleth's honest skepticism, his willingness to question the status quo, should not be lessened in interpretation.

276 N. Lohfink. "Qoheleth 5:17–19—Revelation by Joy." *CBQ* 52 (1990): 625–35.

The "joy of the heart" in verse 19 is "something like divine revelation" (p. 634). A proper understanding of this passage is a key to unlocking the meaning of the book: God is not distant in Ecclesiastes as opposed to the other OT books.

277 R. E. Murphy. "Qohelet and Theology?" *BTB* 21 (1991): 30–33.

Qoheleth's understanding of the fear of God and the activity and work of God show his theology to be within the scope of biblical faith.

278 D. M. Clemens. "The Law of Sin and Death: Ecclesiastes and Genesis 1–3." *Themelios* 19 (1994): 5–8.

Ecclesiastes "is best understood as an arresting but thoroughly orthodox exposition of Genesis 1–3: in both texts, the painful consequences of the fall are central" (p. 5).

279 J. S. Custer. "Qoheleth and the Canon: The Dissenting Voice in Dialogue." *Josephinum Journal of Theology* 1 ns (1994): 15–24.

Qoheleth's views on the human condition are limited in that he has no understanding of the resurrection hope or of prayer.

2.5. Literary Structure and Style

One approach to finding meaning in Ecclesiastes has been to discern the macrostructure of the book. Other studies have dealt with elements of style and specific rhetorical devices, including the possible use of quotations by the author from other works.

2.5.1. Macrostructure

280 H. L. Ginsberg. "The Structure and Contents of the Book of Koheleth." Pp. 138–49 in *Wisdom in Israel and in the Ancient*

Near East: Presented to Professor Harold Henry Rowley. Edited
by M. Noth and D. W. Thomas. VTSup 3. Leiden: E. J. Brill, 1955.
 Building on his previous work (#s 180 and 181), the author
 concludes that the body of the Ecclesiastes contains four divisions. Includes his views on the teaching (more extreme skepticism than Job), date (third century B.C.), and authorship (child
 of his age) of the book.

281 A. D. G. Wright. "The Riddle of the Sphinx: The Structure of the
 Book of Qoheleth." *CBQ* 30 (1968): 313–34. Reprinted in J. L.
 Crenshaw's *Studies in Ancient Israelite Wisdom*. New York:
 KTAV, 1976, pp. 245–66, and in R. B. Zuck's *Reflecting with
 Solomon: Selected Studies on the Book of Ecclesiastes*. Grand
 Rapids: Baker, 1994, pp. 45–65.
 Reviews various attempts to present a coherent structure of
 Ecclesiastes. Author presents an outline of the book based on
 Qoheleth's "train of thought" (p. 325), and a summary of the
 content of the sections. Concludes that the theme of Ecclesi-
 astes is "the idea of the impossibility of understanding what
 God has done" (p. 334). (See also Wright's follow-up articles
 in *CBQ* 42 [1980]: 38–51 and *CBQ* 45 [1983]: 32–43.)

282 M. V. Fox. "Frame-narrative and Composition in the Book of
 Qohelet." *HUCA* 48 (1977): 83–106.
 "[T]he *Book of Qohelet* is to be taken as a whole, as a single,
 well-integrated composition, the product not of editorship but
 of authorship, which uses interplay of voice as a deliberate literary device for rhetorical and artistic purposes" (p. 83).

283 J. A. Loader. *Polar Structures in the Book of Qohelet*. BZAW, 152.
 Berlin/New York: Walter de Gruyter, 1979.
 Polar structures ("patterns of tension created by the counter-
 position of two elements to one another" [p. 1]) are common
 in Qoheleth and show that (1) the author does not borrow from
 Greek philosophy, (2) tensions should not be explained away
 as the work of redactors, and (3) apart from the epilogue, there
 are no contradictions in Ecclesiastes.

284 J. S. M. Mulder. "Qoheleth's Division and Also Its Main Points."
 Pp. 149–59 in *Von Canaan bis Kerala. Festschrift für Prof. Mag.
 Dr. J. P. M. van der Ploeg O. P. zur Vollendung des siebzigsten
 Lebensjahres am 4. Juli 1979*. Edited by W. C. Delsman, J. T.
 Nelis, et al. Verlag Butzon and Bercker Kevelaer, 1982.
 Essentially positive evaluation of Wright's 1968 article (#281).
 Argues that previous interactions with Wright's work have
 not attempted to work out the implications of his conclusions.

285 S. G. Brown. "The Structure of Ecclesiastes." *Evangelical Review of Theology* 14 (1990): 195–208.

Apologetic for the purposefulness of the structure of Ecclesiastes and the importance of understanding meaning as a function of structure. Corroborates the work of Wright (#281).

286 S. de Jong. "A Book on Labour: The Structuring Principles and the Main Theme of the Book of Qohelet." *JSOT* 54 (1992): 107–16.

Ecclesiastes is structured around alternating observation and instruction complexes, the central theme of which is labor. The observations show that all labor is "vanity," while the instructions give advice for careful human behavior.

287 L. Ryken. "Ecclesiastes." Pp. 268–80 in *A Complete Literary Guide to the Bible*. Edited by L. Ryken and T. Longman III. Grand Rapids: Zondervan, 1993.

The book is organized around a contrasting set of opposites, negative statements followed by positive ones. The latter emphasizes the divine perspective.

2.5.2. Stylistic and Rhetorical Devices

288 H. C. Shank. "Qoheleth's World and Life View as Seen in His Recurring Phrases." *Westminster Theological Journal* 37 (1974): 57–73. Reprinted in R. B. Zuck's *Reflecting with Solomon: Selected Studies on the Book of Ecclesiastes*. Grand Rapids: Baker, 1994, pp. 67–80.

Six recurring phrases in Qoheleth demonstrate that the biblical author's worldview is not simply cynical or pessimistic, but a "lucid description of what he can behold in this world and his life which should drive him to seek God" (p. 63).

289 G. S. Ogden. "The 'Better'-Proverb (tôb-Spruch), Rhetorical Criticism, and Qoheleth." *JBL* 96 (1977): 489–505.

Irrespective of the origin of the tôb-*Spruch* genre, it is modified by Qoheleth and functions in the book as a rhetorical device, particularly in affirming death as better than life.

290 E. M. Good. "The Unfilled Sea: Style and Meaning in Ecclesiastes 1:2–11." Pp. 59–73 in *Israelite Wisdom: Theological and Literary Essays in Honor of Samuel Terrien*. Edited by J. G. Gammie et al. Missoula: Scholars, 1978.

Based partly on Gestalt psychology, and using Qoheleth 1:2–11, argues that attention to sentence structure "sharpen[s] the perception of what the text actually says" (p. 61).

291 G. S. Ogden. "Qoheleth's Use of the 'Nothing Is Better' Form." *JBL* 98 (1979): 339–50.

The "nothing is better" form in Qoheleth is used when refer-
ring to the call to enjoy life and its toil, one's God-given lot in
life, and is a response to the refrain, "what does it profit a man?"

292 M. V. Fox. "The Identification of Quotations in Biblical Literature." *ZAW* 92 (1980): 416–31.
Focusing on Ecclesiastes and Job, the author establishes cri-
teria for identifying the presence of quotations. Proper identification of certain passages as quotations is essential for a
proper understanding of the author's intention.

293 R. N. Whybray. "The Identification and Use of Quotations in
Ecclesiastes." Pp. 435–51 in *Congress Volume: Vienna, 1980.*
VTSup 32. Leiden: E. J. Brill, 1981. Reprinted in R. B. Zuck's
*Reflecting with Solomon: Selected Studies on the Book of Eccle-
siastes.* Grand Rapids: Baker, 1994, pp. 185–99.
Qoheleth's use of quotations from earlier wisdom works as
providing insight into Qoheleth's relationship to earlier wisdom literature, especially Proverbs 10–29. Qoheleth essentially saw himself as a wisdom writer in the Israelite tradition. He quotes Proverbs approvingly, although he emphasizes
folly's prevailing over wisdom.

294 A. R. Ceresko. "The Function of Antanaclasis (ms' "to find" ms
"to reach, overtake, grasp") in Hebrew Poetry, Especially in the
Book of Qoheleth." *CBQ* 44 (1982): 551–69.
Argues that the author of Ecclesiastes employs the rhetorical
device antanaclasis (repetition of the same word with a different meaning).

295 G. S. Ogden. "The Mathematics of Wisdom: Qoheleth IV 1–12."
VT 34 (1984): 446–53.
Qoheleth combines the numerical saying form with the tôb-
Spruch, a combination found nowhere else in the OT.

296 I. J. J. Spangenberg. "Quotations in Ecclesiastes: An Appraisal."
Old Testament Essays 4 (1991): 19–35.
Summarizes previous scholarship and examines four passages
in Ecclesiastes with respect to the presence of quotations. Cri-
teria for identification of quotations in Ecclesiastes are in a
state of flux.

297 O. Loretz. "Poetry and Prose in the Book of Qohelet (1:1–3:22;
7:23–8:1; 9:6–10; 12:8–14). Pp. 155–89 in *Verse in Ancient Near
Eastern Prose.* Edited by J. C. de Moor and W. G. E. Watson.
Neukirchener Verlag, 1993.

Contrary to prevalent scholarly opinion, Qoheleth is not an essentially poetic composition that tolerates the presence of prose. Rather, poetic sections are inserted within the prose. The prose sections are Qoheleth's while the poetic insertions are those of a postexilic traditionalist wanting to "curb" Qoheleth's radical thinking.

2.6. Translation and Interpretation

298 G. R. Driver. "Problems and Solutions." *VT* 4 (1954): 225–45.
Discussion of some difficult words and phrases in Qoheleth (and Esther), some LXX translational curiosities, and assonance.

299 S. Holm-Nielsen. "The Book of Ecclesiastes and the Interpretation of It in Jewish and Christian Theology." *Annual of the Swedish Theological Institute* 10 (1975–76): 38–96.
On the interpretive nature of all translations, specifically the LXX, Peshitta, Vulgate translations of Ecclesiastes. Also discusses rabbinic evidence. (See earlier, briefer version in *VT* 24 [1974]: 168–77.)

300 R. E. Murphy. "Qoheleth Interpreted: The Bearing of the Past on the Present." *VT* 32 (1982): 331–37.
Brief review of the role of the interpreter's presuppositions in the history of Jewish and Christian interpretation of Qoheleth, in part, to help modern interpreters examine their own presuppositions.

301 R. E. Murphy. "On Translating Ecclesiastes." *CBQ* 53 (1991): 571–79.
Discussion of several dubious or ambiguous passages for which the MT is clearly the only or better reading to highlight the many difficulties the translator of Ecclesiastes faces.

302 P. Machinist. "Fate, *miqreh*, and Reason: Some Reflections on Qohelet and Biblical Thought." Pp. 159–75 in *Solving Riddles and Untying Knots: Biblical, Epigraphic, and Semitic Studies in Honor of Jonas C. Greenfield*. Edited by Z. Zevit, S. Gitin, and M. Sokoloff. Winona Lake, Ind.: Eisenbrauns, 1995.
Death is the central notion for understanding the concept of fate in Qoheleth. The use of rationality suggests possible connections to Greek culture.

3. Job

The problems that arise in any academic study of Job are similar to those that affect the other wisdom books, particularly its origins (including possible ANE influence). The unity of the book has been routinely questioned; the narrative prose sections (chaps. 1–2 and 42:7–17) are thought to be later additions to the dialogues and speeches that form the heart of the book. Also, Job raises, at least for some, troubling notions about suffering and God's justice. Just as Job's persistent plea of innocence confounded the advice of his friends, the book today also flies in the face of conventional wisdom and hence continues to captivate and provoke a broad spectrum of readers.

3.1. Anthologies and Introductions

303 P. S. Sanders (ed.). *Twentieth Century Interpretations of the Book of Job: A Collection of Critical Essays.* Englewood Cliffs, N.J.: Prentice-Hall, 1955.

Includes several essays on topics of traditional scholarly interest (e.g., purpose of the book, meter) as well as the book's literary qualities (see §3.5).

304 H. H. Rowley. "The Book of Job and Its Meaning." *Bulletin of the John Rylands University Library of Manchester* 41 (1958–59): 167–207.

Overview of many critical problems that face the interpreter of Job and the solutions that scholars have proposed. Job teaches that the pious have God, which is far more than the prosperity of the wicked.

305 R. E. Hone (ed.). *The Voice out of the Whirlwind: The Book of Job.* San Francisco: Chandler, 1960.
Collection of previously published essays on introductions to Job; sermons on Job; drawings and poetry; modern dramatic adaptations.

306 J. Paterson. *The Wisdom of Israel: Job and Proverbs.* London and Nashville: Lutterworth and Abingdon, 1961.
Popular, nontechnical overview of "purpose, plan, exposition, and power" of Job and Proverbs.

307 R. Gordis. *The Book of God and Man: A Study of Job.* Chicago: University of Chicago Press, 1963.
Seventeen essays on a variety of topics concerning the study of Job (e.g., cultural background, language, ANE literature). Includes translation with introductory comments for each section.

308 N. H. Snaith. *The Book of Job: Its Origin and Purpose.* Studies in Biblical Theology. Second Series, 11. London: SCM, 1968.
Section-by-section summary of Job with discussion of various critical issues. Original book did not include any of the speeches of the three friends or Elihu or chapter 28. The story is a folk-tale. Comparison with ANE literature.

309 N. N. Glatzer (ed.). *The Dimensions of Job: A Study and Selected Readings.* New York: Schocken, 1969.
Selected modern readings of Job: Jewish, Christian, humanist. Includes essays on theodicy, mystery, and faith.

310 J. Barr. "The Book of Job and Its Modern Interpreters." *Bulletin of the John Rylands University Library of Manchester* 54 (1971): 28–46.
Overview of the book of Job with an analysis of four recent trends in scholarship: vocabulary and grammar, comparative method, reconstruction of the original form of the book, literary approach.

311 W. E. Aufrecht (ed.). *Studies in the Book of Job.* Studies in Religion Supplement, 16. Waterloo, Ont.: Wilfrid Laurier University Press, 1985.

Four essays by R. J. Williams, P. C. Craigie, C. E. Cox, and W. E. Aufrecht on current trends in scholarship, and the relevance of Ugaritic, LXX, and Aramaic studies to the book of Job.

312 D. Robertson. "Job and Ecclesiastes." *Soundings* 73 (1990): 257–72.

Job and Qoheleth attempt to find order in chaos. Life consists of "a sequence of 'seasons' juxtaposed, of accumulated 'times' that must be lived one at a time" (p. 272).

313 L. G. Perdue and W. C. Gilpin. *The Voice from the Whirlwind: Interpreting the Book of Job.* Nashville: Abingdon, 1992.

Thirteen essays on a variety of topics, including history of interpretation and contemporary theological reflection. First five essays treat nature of God as presented in Job, problem of evil, Job and folk literature, Job and inner-biblical discourse.

314 R. B. Zuck (ed.). *Sitting with Job: Selected Studies on the Book of Job.* Grand Rapids: Baker, 1992.

Collection of thirty-four previously published essays, many of which appeared originally as chapters in monographs and commentaries. Organized under two headings: overviews of the book and specific themes/passages.

315 C. A. Newsom. "Considering Job." *Currents in Research: Biblical Studies* 1 (1993): 87–118.

Select overview of commentaries and works on a number of topics. Notes the increase of literary approaches.

316 W. A. M. Beuken (ed.). *The Book of Job.* BETL, 114. Leuven: Leuven University Press, 1994.

Collection of twenty-eight papers given at the Colloquium Biblicum Lovaniense XLII on August 24–26, 1993. Includes essays in German, French, and English on a wide variety of topics.

317 C. A. Newsom. "Job and Ecclesiastes." Pp. 177–94 in *Old Testament Interpretation: Past Present and Future.* Edited by J. L. Mays, D. L. Peterson, and K. H. Richards. Nashville: Abingdon, 1995.

Emphasizes current focus on Job as a literary product. Ecclesiastes research is still dominated by classical critical questions (e.g., distinctive language, relation to Hellenistic culture, biblical theology).

❡ **318** D. Wolfers. *Deep Things out of Darkness: The Book of Job*. Grand
Rapids: Eerdmans, 1995.
>New translation preceded by more than three hundred pages
>of introductory comments ("The Art of Mistranslation,"
>provenance) and other matters (identity of Job, the wicked,
>Behemoth and Leviathan, Job's comforters, Satan; Deutero-
>nomic covenant; nature of Job's illness; speech-cycles).

❡ **319** Y. Hoffman. *A Blemished Perfection: The Book of Job in Context*. JSOTSup 213. Sheffield: Sheffield Academic, 1996.
>Literary, linguistic, and theological investigation in the con-
>text of the OT and the ANE. The "perfection" of the book of
>Job is seen paradoxically in its imperfections, both with respect
>to "Job as a believer and to the literary character of the book
>itself" (p. 9).

3.2. Origins and ANE Influence

As with most of the biblical books treated in this volume, the question of origins and ANE influence loom large over the scholarly land-
scape. Unlike the other books, however, there still remains little consensus over whether the book of Job can be tied directly to any ANE
text or even genre. For some, it is unique among ANE laments. This
section also includes works that discuss the possible influence of
Northwest Semitic on Job, although this influence is primarily linguistic and not on the level of content or theology.

3.2.1. Job and Israelite Religion

320 M. Jastrow *The Book of Job: Its Origin, Growth, and Interpretation*. Philadelphia and London: Lippincott, 1920.
>Discussion of various strata and stages that went into trans-
>forming the skeptical folklore of Job into the orthodox book
>of Job. Includes section on Job as philosophy and literature,
>and the author's own translation.

321 N. M. Sarna. "Epic Substratum in the Prose of Job." *JBL* 76 (1957):
13–25.
>"The considerable amount of epic substratum indicates that
>our present narrative framework is directly derived from an
>ancient [i.e., patriarchal] Epic of Job" (p. 25).

322 R. Polzin and D. Robertson. *Studies in the Book of Job*. Semeia,
7. Missoula: Scholars, 1977.

Seven articles (including responses) that deal with comedy and irony in Job (see 3.5).

323 J. G. Janzen. "The Place of the Book of Job in the History of Israel's Religion." Pp. 523–37 in *Ancient Israelite Religion: Essays in Honor of Frank Moore Cross*. Edited by P. D. Miller Jr. et al. Philadelphia: Fortress, 1987.

Building on insights made previously by T. Jacobsen and F. M. Cross, Janzen stresses the "fundamental continuity" (p. 526) of Job's theodicy with biblical tradition.

324 D. J. A. Clines. "Deconstructing the Book of Job." Pp. 106–23 in *What Does Eve Do to Help? And Other Readerly Questions to the Old Testament*. Edited by D. J. A. Clines. JSOTSup 94. Sheffield: JSOT, 1990.

Job's readership consists of literate, wealthy, intellectual men. It cannot speak to the poor or to women. See also the author's article in *Bible Review* 11, no. 2 (1995): 30–35, 43–44, and in W. A. M. Beuken's *The Book of Job* (#316).

325 E. F. Davis. "Job and Jacob: The Integrity of Faith." Pp. 203–24 in *Reading between Texts: Intertextuality and the Hebrew Bible*. Edited by D. N. Fewell. Louisville: Westminster/John Knox, 1992.

Job and the Jacob narrative (both Job and Jacob are called "blameless" [*tam*]) are to be read together in the context of the crisis of the exile.

326 D. Wolfers. "Job: A Universal Drama." *JBQ* 21 (1993): 13–23, 80–89.

Job symbolizes Israel's suffering under Sennacherib.

3.2.2. ANE Influence

327 M. Jastrow. "A Babylonian Parallel to the Story of Job." *JBL* 25 (1906): 135–91.

Story of Tâbi-utul-Bêl of Nippur who, like, Job comments on the sufferings inflicted on him. It is a didactic piece aimed at the problem of evil, which may be indirectly connected to the biblical Job.

328 S. N. Kramer. "'Man and His God': A Sumerian Variation on the 'Job' Motif." Pp. 170–82 in *Wisdom in Israel and in the Ancient Near East: Presented to Professor Harold Henry Rowley*. Edited by M. Noth and D. W. Thomas. VTSup 3. Leiden: E. J. Brill, 1955.

Text and translation of an early-second-millennium B.C. text that resembles the book of Job.

329 G. von Rad. "Job xxxviii and Ancient Egyptian Wisdom." *The Problem of the Hexateuch and Other Essays*, pp. 281–91. Translated by E. W. Trueman Dicken. Edinburgh/London: Oliver & Boyd, 1966. Original Title: *Gesammelte Studien zum Alten Testament*. München: C. Kaiser, 1958/73.

Shows parallels between Job 38 and the *Onomasticon* of Amenope and *Papyrus Anastasi I*.

330 W. A. Irwin. "Job's Redeemer." *JBL* 81 (1962): 217–29.

The figure of the "redeemer" in Job in its ANE context. The precise identification remains ambiguous.

331 J. Murtagh. "The Book of Job and the Book of the Dead." *Irish Theological Quarterly* 35 (1968): 166–73.

The "weighing of the heart of the deceased" as judgment in the Egyptian *Book of the Dead* is clearly repeated in Job, thus arguing for the dependence of the latter on the former.

332 J. Gray. "The Book of Job in the Context of Near Eastern Literature." *ZAW* 82 (1970): 251–69.

The book of Job is reminiscent of Mesopotamian texts concerning the suffering of the righteous.

333 E. B. Smick. "Mythology in the Book of Job." *Journal of the Evangelical Theological Society* 13 (1970): 101–8. Reprinted in R. B. Zuck's *Sitting with Job: Selected Studies on the Book of Job*. Grand Rapids: Baker, 1992, pp. 221–29. (See also E. B. Smick. "Another Look at the Mythological Elements in the Book of Job." *Westminster Theological Journal* 40 [1978]: 213–28. Reprinted in R. B. Zuck's *Sitting with Job: Selected Studies on the Book of Job*. Grand Rapids: Baker, 1992, pp. 231–44.)

Similarities in language and descriptive metaphors between Job and ANE mythology do not suggest that Israel's God shared in the same limitations as the numerous gods of Israel's neighbors.

334 J. J. M. Roberts. "Job and the Israelite Religious Tradition." *ZAW* 89 (1977): 107–14.

The precise historical background of the book of Job is difficult to determine and may not be relevant for the interpretation of this piece of literature.

335 R. G. Albertson. "Job and Ancient Near Eastern Wisdom Literature." Pp. 213–30 in *Scripture in Context II: More Essays on the Comparative Method*. Edited by W. W. Hallo et al. Winona Lake, Ind.: Eisenbrauns, 1983.

Very brief overview of ten elements of the book of Job, including relevant material in biblical and extrabiblical literature.

336 M. Weinfeld. "Job and Its Mesopotamian Parallels—A Typological Analysis." Pp. 217–26 in *Text and Context: Old Testament Studies for F. C. Fensham*. Edited by W. Claassen. JSOTSup 48. Sheffield: JSOT, 1988.

Mesopotamian stories that seem to parallel Job are actually liturgies of thanksgiving of the sufferer (they are written in the first person and they begin and end with praise). Job is simply the story of a righteous sufferer.

337 G. L. Mattingly. "The Pious Sufferer: Mesopotamia's Traditional Theodicy and Job's Counselors." Pp. 305–48 in *The Bible in the Light of Cuneiform Literature: Scripture in Context III*. Edited by W. W. Hallo et al. Ancient Near Eastern Texts and Studies, 8. Lewiston: Mellon, 1990.

The words of Job's counselors exhibit a theodicy similar to that found in the Sumerian story known as *Man and His God*: a reaffirmation of the "trustworthiness of their traditional dogmas concerning sin and suffering vis-à-vis the undeniable reality of human suffering" (p. 311).

338 Y. Hoffman. "Ancient Near Eastern Literary Conventions and the Restoration of Job." *ZAW* 103 (1991): 399–411.

Past attempts to "restore" the book of Job have not taken sufficient account of ANE literary conventions. Job's difficult and obscure vocabulary and sense of artistry argue strongly for the book's authenticity. The book's dialogic and cyclical structure has extrabiblical parallels.

3.2.3. Linguistic Analysis

339 G. R. Driver. "Problems in the Hebrew Text of Job." Pp. 72–93 in *Wisdom in Israel and in the Ancient Near East: Presented to Professor Harold Henry Rowley*. Edited by M. Noth and D. W. Thomas. VTSup 3. Leiden: E. J. Brill, 1955.

Twenty-six problematic passages are treated "with the hope of solving a few of the many difficulties in the book of Job or alternatively, where a proposed solution does not commend itself, of offering something which may ultimately lead others to their correct interpretation" (p. 72).

340 A. Blommerde. *Northwest Semitic Grammar and Job*. Biblica et Orientalia, 22. Rome: Pontifical Biblical Institute, 1969.

Overview of the characteristics of Northwest Semitic grammar, followed by numerous examples of such characteristics throughout Job.

341 L. L. Grabbe. *Comparative Philology and the Text of Job: A Study in Methodology.* SBLDS, 34. Missoula: Scholars, 1977.
Application of J. Barr's methodology (*Comparative Philology and the Text of the Old Testament*) to Job.

342 A. R. Ceresko. *Job 29–31 in Light of Northwest Semitic: A Translation and Philological Commentary.* Biblica et Orientalia, 36. Rome: Pontifical Biblical Institute, 1980.
Builds on work by M. Pope (*Job*, Anchor Bible Commentary 15) and A. Blommerde (#340). Includes extensive bibliography and indexes (a grammar of Job 29–31 and lists of parallel word pairs).

343 W. L. Michel. *Job in the Light of Northwest Semitic*, Vol. 1. Biblica et Orientalia, 42. Rome: Biblical Institute, 1987.
Treats Job 1:1–14:22. Philological commentary on Job in its Northwest Semitic context. Follows on work of M. Dahood.

3.3. Theology/Teaching

Legitimate questions have been raised concerning the extent to which Job can be classified as wisdom literature (not to mention what the classification "wisdom literature" itself means). Does not Job's subversion of the "traditional" wisdom espoused by his friends indicate the inadequacy of "wisdom" as a category to describe the book of Job? Also, what continues to be a popular topic in scholarship is how the book handles the problem of suffering and of God's justice in the world.

3.3.1. Job and Wisdom

344 P. P. Zerafa. *The Wisdom of God in the Book of Job.* Studia Universitatis S. Thomae in Urbe. Rome: Herder, 1978.
Study of wisdom in Job, primarily by means of a detailed study of its composition and texts that speak of God's wisdom, in order to "trace the historical emergence of a divine wisdom in Israel's cultural tradition."

345 N. C. Habel. "Of Things Beyond Me: Wisdom in the Book of Job." *Currents in Theology and Mission* 10 (1983): 142–54. Reprinted in R. B. Zuck's *Sitting with Job: Selected Studies on the Book of Job*. Grand Rapids: Baker, 1992, pp. 303–15.

346 R. Albertz. "The Sage and Pious Wisdom in the Book of Job: The Friends' Perspective." Pp. 243–61 in *The Sage in Israel and the Ancient Near East*. Edited by J. G. Gammie and L. G. Perdue. Winona Lake, Ind.: Eisenbrauns, 1990.

The author describes the theology of wisdom embodied by Job's friends as "a conscious synthesis of the sapiential mastering of life and piety, or as reason's permeation of personal piety, fashioned by the perspective of the upper class" (p. 260). It is flawed in that it "seeks to penetrate and explain the living relationship of God and humanity in a rational manner" (p. 261).

347 S. Terrien. "Job as a Sage." Pp. 231–42 in *The Sage in Israel and the Ancient Near East*. Edited by J. G. Gammie and L. G. Perdue. Winona Lake, Ind.: Eisenbrauns, 1990.

Discusses the possible portrait of Job as a sage by examining wisdom vocabulary in Job, the presence of proverbial sayings, sapiential themes, his "unconventional" brand of wisdom.

348 K. J. Dell. *The Book of Job as Skeptical Literature*. Berlin/New York: Walter de Gruyter, 1991.

Traditional and critical interpretations of Job. "Parody" rather than traditional labels (e.g., wisdom) is the best genre classification. A skeptical tradition (Hellenistic influence) best accounts for the author's "suspension of belief" (p. 215).

349 L. G. Perdue. *Wisdom in Revolt: Metaphorical Theology in the Book of Job*. JSOTSup 112. Sheffield: Almond, 1991. (See also pp. 129–56 in Beuken [#316].)

Job employs common ANE metaphors used to express creation theology, that is, divine action (procreation, artistry, word, battle) and anthropology (ruler, slave). "In [his] quest for the articulation of meaning, Job moves through a series of collapsing and emerging worlds, ending with another deconstruction of mythic reality, but also the promising beginnings of new creation" (p. 269). Wisdom in Job, as seen in chapter 28, means "governing principle" or "design." Job cannot discern the seeming injustice of his suffering because the design is hidden. Job does not acquire this wisdom; he gains a knowledge of God instead.

350 L. G. Perdue. "Wisdom in the Book of Job." Pp. 73–98 in *In Search of Wisdom: Essays in Memory of John G. Gammie*. Edited by L. G. Perdue et al. Louisville: Westminster/John Knox, 1993.

Wisdom in Job is expressed in three categories evident in wisdom in general: wisdom as knowing (poetic portions), discipline (narrative portions), world-construction (ultimately limited by the mystery of God).

3.3.2. Suffering

351 B. Blake. *The Book of Job and the Problem of Suffering*. London: Hodder & Stoughton, 1911.

Translation and summary of the content and teaching of each of the major divisions of Job.

352 D. Cox. *The Triumph of Impotence: Job and the Tradition of the Absurd*. Analecta Gregoriana, 212. Rome: Gregorian, 1978.

The problem posed in Job is the absurdity of human existence. Job finds that creation is irrational and God is arbitrary. Faith is "submission to unreason" (p. 157), which clears the path to authentic existence.

353 J. G. Gammie. "Behemoth and Leviathan: On the Didactic and Theological Significance of Job 40:15–41:26." Pp. 217–31 in *Israelite Wisdom: Theological and Literary Essays in Honor of Samuel Terrien*. Edited by J. G. Gammie et al. Missoula: Scholars, 1978.

God's second discourse (40:6–41:26) does not primarily illustrate God's power and majesty. Rather, these beasts are didactic elements that speak directly to Job's suffering. "Seeming to portray Job's inability to conquer such marvelously wrought beasts as Behemoth and Leviathan, the beasts themselves celebrate instead Job's triumph" (p. 226).

354 P. Kreeft. "Job: Life as Suffering." Pp. 59–95 in Kreeft's *Three Philosophies of Life*. San Francisco: Ignatius, 1989.

God will bring good out of evil. One must be patient (silent) for resolution. Job learned to long for God.

355 T. W. Tilley. "God and the Silencing of Job." *Modern Theology* 5 (1989): 257–70.

Job should not be read as a theodicy. The Readers of Job have a choice, either to read Job "as silencing the voice of the suffering or . . . allow Job to silence their claims about how God and suffering are related" (p. 267).

356 A. G. Hunter. "Could Not the Universe Have Come into Existence 200 Yards to the Left? A Thematic Study of Job." Pp. 140–59
in *Text as Pretext: Essays in Honour of Robert Davidson.*
JSOTSup 138. Edited by R. P. Carroll. Sheffield: JSOT, 1992.
Job is not so much a theodicy as a statement of the individual's suffering in the context of a community of faith.

357 F. C. Hyman. "Job, or the Suffering God." *Judaism* 42 (1993):
218–28.
God's "suffering" can be seen, for example, in his challenge
from Satan.

358 O. Leaman. *Evil and Suffering in Jewish Philosophy.* Cambridge
Studies in Religious Traditions, 6. Cambridge: Cambridge University Press, 1995.
The problem of evil presented in Job and by various Jewish
thinkers including Philo, Saadya Gaon, Spinoza, M. Buber,
and since the Holocaust.

3.3.3. Retribution and God's Justice

359 M. Tsevat. "The Meaning of the Book of Job." *HUCA* 37 (1966):
73–106. Reprinted in J. L. Crenshaw's *Studies in Ancient Israelite
Wisdom.* New York: KTAV, 1976, pp. 341–74; and in R. B. Zuck's
Sitting with Job: Selected Studies on the Book of Job. Grand
Rapids: Baker, 1992, pp. 189–229.
Offers some defense of the authenticity of the final chapters
of Job, which constitute God's answer to Job. This answer is
a repudiation of the notion of fair retribution, an assumption
that lies at the heart of both Job's and his friends' speeches.

360 J. Faur. "Reflections on Job and Situation-Morality." *Judaism* 19
(1970): 219–25.
"[T]he objective of *Job* is not to justify the Ways of the Lord—
for these need no justification—but, rather, to examine the
grounds of morality" (p. 219). Universally valid morality is
impracticable, hence, "the claim of universal morality is
reducible to that of situation-morality" (p. 225).

361 M. V. Fox. "Job 38 and God's Rhetoric." *Semeia* 19 (1981): 53–61.
The purpose of God's speech is to overwhelm Job, to say to
him, "You know very well that I and I alone created order and
maintain it in the world, and I know that you know, and you
know that I know that you know" (p. 60).

362 S. H. Scholnick. "The Meaning of *Mispat* in the Book of Job." *JBL* 101 (1982): 521–29. Reprinted in R. B. Zuck's *Sitting with Job: Selected Studies on the Book of Job*. Grand Rapids: Baker, 1992, pp. 349–58.

The meaning of *Mispat* changes from juridical (court) justice to executive (sovereign) justice as the book of Job progresses. Job learns that "the divinely ordained justice in the world is God's governance" (p. 529).

363 J. C. L. Gibson. "On Evil in the Book of Job." Pp. 399–419 in *Ascribe to the Lord: Biblical and Other Studies in Memory of Peter C. Craigie*. Edited by L. Eslinger and Glen Taylor. JSOTSup 67. Sheffield: JSOT, 1988.

Job's questioning of God in the final chapters. Behemoth and Leviathan are metaphors for Satan (chap. 1), whom God must keep "in subjection and prevent . . . from bringing to nought all that he has created" (p. 417).

364 J. T. Wilcox. *The Bitterness of Job: A Philosophical Reading*. Ann Arbor: University of Michigan Press, 1989.

"[T]he message of the whole book is deeply skeptical, agnostic, suspicious of man's claims to insight into the highest mysteries"; the proper response is "intellectual humility and silence" (p. 173).

365 S. E. Porter. "The Message of the Book of Job: Job 42:7b as Key to Interpretation?" *Evangelical Quarterly* 63, no. 4 (1991): 291–304.

"Job is . . . right to question the God and universe that seem to visit evil upon those who act morally and justly" (p. 302).

366 S. Bakon. "God and Man on Trial." *JBQ* 21 (1993): 226–35.

Job shows us that evil in the world is a necessary element for making moral decisions.

367 T. F. Dailey. *The Repentant Job: A Ricoeurian Icon for Biblical Theology*. Lanham, Md.: University Press of America, 1994. (See also "The Aesthetics of Repentance: Re-Reading the Phenomenon of Job." *BTB* 23 [1993]: 64–70.)

"[E]ngagement with the text . . . will allow readers of the Book of Job greater access to the depth of its meaning" (p. 5). "In 42:2–6, Job repents of the need for absolute rational certainty with regard to the meaning of [human] existence" (p. 186).

368 J. D. Pleins. "Why Do You Hide Your Face?" *Int* 48 (1994): 229–38.

God is silent while Job debates with his friends. He speaks in
the end to assure Job that he will console him and bring him
out of his suffering.

369 L. Wilson. "The Book of Job and the Fear of God." *TynBul* 46
(1995): 59–79.
The "fear of God" concept in Job is the same as the "fear of
Yahweh" concept in Proverbs. Maintaining such fear, however, does not provide his much-needed comfort.

3.4. Literary Structure, Genre, and Meaning

The fact that the book of Job is divided somewhat neatly between
prose narratives that frame the book as a whole and the intervening dialogues and speeches, written in poetic form, has led to a virtual consensus that the two parts were written at different times. More specifically, the narrative portions are thought by many to have been written
at a later time and then appended to the poetic section (the "original"
Job) in order to sanitize its less "orthodox" teachings. But as the cita-
tions below indicate, the debate is not over. The book has also enjoyed
its share of poetic analyses, as have the other biblical books of similar
genres.

3.4.1. Macrostructure and Genre

370 C. Westermann. *The Structure of the Book of Job: A Form-
Critical Analysis.* Translated by C. A. Muenchow. Philadelphia:
Fortress, 1981. Original Title: *Der Aufbau des Buches Hiob.*
Beiträge zur historischen Theologie, 23. Tübingen: J. C. B. Mohr
(Paul Siebeck), 1956.
Job is a lamentation. The key to unlocking the meaning of the
book is the "basic recognition" that Job's suffering is "developed along three axes which determine human existence in
general—the self in isolation [Job], the self over against other
human beings [Job's friends], and the self over against God"
(p. vii).

371 R. Gordis. "Elihu the Intruder: A Study of the Authenticity of
Job (Chapters 32–33)." Pp. 60–78 in *Biblical and Other Studies.*
Edited by A. Altman. Cambridge, Mass.: Harvard University
Press, 1963.
Reviews arguments against the authenticity of the Elihu
speeches. Concludes that "the Elihu section emanates from
the same author writing at a later period in his life" (p. 72).

372 R. M. Polzin. *Biblical Structuralism: Method and Subjectivity in the Study of Ancient Texts.* Philadelphia: Fortress, 1977.

Structural analysis of Job. The whirlwind experience teaches Job that "faith in redemption of some sort is once again possible . . . and he could now see his way to a belief he had once lost" (p. 121).

373 J. G. Williams. "Deciphering the Unspoken: The Theophany of Job." *HUCA* 49 (1978): 59–72. Reprinted in R. B. Zuck's *Sitting with Job: Selected Studies on the Book of Job.* Grand Rapids: Baker, 1992, pp. 359–72.

Subtle connection between the speeches of God and the rest of the book lies in the irony of what is left unexpressed or omitted. Job is a comedy.

374 J. A. Baker. "The Book of Job: Unity and Meaning." *Studia Biblica 1978: I. Papers on Old Testament and Related Themes.* Edited by E. A. Livingstone. Sixth International Congress on Biblical Studies. JSOTSup 11. Sheffield: JSOT, 1979.

Job must be understood in its present final form; it is of postexilic origin; the message of the whole transcends that of the particular parts.

375 J. F. A. Sawyer. "The Authorship and Structure of the Book of Job." Pp. 253–57 in *Studia Biblica 1978: I. Papers on Old Testament and Related Themes.* Edited by E. A. Livingstone. Sixth International Congress on Biblical Studies. JSOTSup 11. Sheffield: JSOT, 1979.

Job is the product of "creative composition rather than arbitrary compilation" (p. 253). The symmetry of the book breaks down at the end of the third cycle of speeches, which "focuses the reader's attention on the futility of the dialogue between Job and God" (p. 33).

376 G. W. Parsons. "Literary Features of the Book of Job." *BSac* 138 (1981): 213–29. Reprinted in R. B. Zuck's *Sitting with Job: Selected Studies on the Book of Job.* Grand Rapids: Baker, 1992, pp. 35–49.

No one genre category sufficiently explains the book of Job. It is lawsuit, lament, and controversy dialogue. Two main literary devices, irony and mythopoeic language, are employed to neutralize the ANE dogma of retribution.

377 G. W. Parsons. "The Structure and Purpose of the Book of Job." *BSac* 138 (1981): 139–57. Reprinted in R. B. Zuck's *Sitting with*

Job: Selected Studies on the Book of Job. Grand Rapids: Baker, 1992, pp. 17–33.

378   D. J. A. Clines. "The Arguments of Job's Three Friends." Pp. 199–214 in *Art and Meaning: Rhetoric in Biblical Literature.* Edited by D. J. A. Clines et al. JSOTSup 19. Sheffield: JSOT, 1982. Reprinted in R. B. Zuck's *Sitting with Job: Selected Studies on the Book of Job.* Grand Rapids: Baker, 1992, pp. 265–81.
      Study of the rhetorical devices in the speech cycles of Job's friends (tonality, nodal sentences, topoi, verb modality). Argues also for the coherence of these speeches as well as their distinctiveness.

379   D. Cox. "A Rational Inquiry into God: Chapters 4–27 of the Book of Job." *Gregorianum* 67, no. 4 (1986): 621–58.
      Chapters 4–27 are an "identifiable unit" (a dispute) that is "framed by two thematic monologues: chapter 3 and chapters 29–31" and "makes up one panel of a diptych that effectively constitutes the book: Job 3–31, a poetic dialogue; and Job 38–42, a divine response" (p. 621).

380   E. B. Smick. "Architectonics, Structured Poems, and Rhetorical Devices in the Book of Job." Pp. 87–104 in *A Tribute to Gleason Archer.* Edited by W. C. Kaiser and R. F. Youngblood. Chicago: Moody, 1986.
      Structure and rhetorical devices bring coherence to the book of Job and are tied to the book's theology.

381   C. Fontaine. "Folklore Structure in the Book of Job: A Formalist Reading." Pp. 205–32 in *Directions in Biblical Hebrew Poetry.* Edited by E. R. Follis. JSOTSup 40. Sheffield: JSOT, 1987.
      "A structural analysis of Job confirms that, taken as a whole, the work may be considered a 'poeticized folktale'" (p. 223).

382   D. Wolfers. "Elihu: The Provenance and Content of His Speech." *Dor le Dor* 16 (1987–88): 90–98.
      "The Elihu speeches are an integral part of the original Book of Job, composed by the author of the rest of the work at the same time to fulfill an essential function [Elihu becomes a spokesmen for Job to God]" (p. 98).

383   R. W. E. Forrest. "The Two Faces of Job: Imagery and Integrity in the Prologue." Pp. 385–98 in *Ascribe to the Lord: Biblical and Other Studies in Memory of Peter C. Craigie.* Edited by L. Eslinger and Glen Taylor. JSOTSup 67. Sheffield: JSOT, 1988.

Contrary to current popular opinion that the prologue (chaps. 1–2) and the dialogue (chaps. 3–31) were originally separate, the author argues that "certain key words and phrases" (p. 385) in chapters 1–2 anticipate Job's apparent about-face in chapter 3.

384 J. E. Miller. "The Vision of Eliphaz as Foreshadowing in the Book of Job." *Proceedings, Eastern Great Lakes Biblical Society* 9 (1989): 98–112.

Eliphaz's first speech (4:12–21) foreshadows the theophany from the whirlwind as a "revelatory source of wisdom" (p. 110). The Eliphaz speech denigrates creation while the whirlwind speech upholds traditional wisdom's respect for creation and order in the universe.

385 J. A. Gladson. "Job." Pp. 230–44 in *A Complete Literary Guide to the Bible*. Edited by L. Ryken and T. Longman III. Grand Rapids: Zondervan, 1993.

Job defies a single genre classification. Narrative and poetic portions create a tension that raises the key question: What is God like? Overview of poetic style.

386 D. Wolfers. "The Speech-Cycles in the Book of Job." *VT* 43 (1993): 385–402.

There are only two speech-cycles in Job, but the common consensus that the alleged third speech is corrupt is wrong.

387 J. E. Course. *Speech and Response: A Rhetorical Analysis of the Introductions to the Speeches of the Book of Job (Chaps. 4–24)*. CBQMS, 25. Washington, D.C.: CBA, 1994.

Explication of the literary connections (word repetition, allusion) among the various speeches between Job and his friends.

388 D. E. Fleming. "Job: The Tale of Patient Faith and the Book of God's Dilemma." *VT* 44 (1994): 468–82.

The dialogue between Satan and God is an addition to the original story. It provides the framework for the prose and poetic sections.

389 P. L. Redditt. "Reading the Speech Cycles in the Book of Job." *HAR* 14 (1994): 205–14.

"The third cycle [chaps. 22–31] presents Job as wavering in his convictions, considering whether to adopt the views of his 'friends'" (pp. 205–6). This sheds light on the Elihu speech and the dialogue with God that follows.

3.4.2. Poetic Structure

390 C. L. Feinberg. "The Poetic Structure of the Book of Job and the Ugaritic Literature." *BSac* 103 (1946): 283–92.

> The poetry of Job and that of Ugarit are similar in a number of features.

391 W. A. Irwin. "Poetic Structure and the Dialogue of Job." *Journal of Near Eastern Studies* 5 (1946): 26–39.

> The book of Job exhibits a striking uniformity in poetic structure throughout.

392 P. Skehan. "Strophic Patterns in the Book of Job." *CBQ* 23 (1961): 125–42. Reprinted in Skehan's *Studies in Israelite Poetry and Wisdom*. CBQMS, 1. Washington, D.C.: Catholic Biblical Association, 1971, pp. 96–113.

> No analysis of Job can commence without first establishing its strophic structure. Also suggests that such an analysis may help provide a framework for making text-critical decisions.

393 P. Skehan. "Job's Final Plea (Job 29–31) and the Lord's Reply (Job 38–41)." *Bib* 45 (1964): 51–61. Reprinted in Skehan's *Studies in Israelite Poetry and Wisdom*. CBQMS, 1. Washington, D.C.: Catholic Biblical Association, 1971, pp. 114–23.

> A strophic analysis of this portion of Job following on the author's previous work (#392).

394 M. J. Dahood. "Chiasmus in Job: A Text-Critical and Philological Criterion." Pp. 119–30 in *A Light unto My Path: Old Testament Studies in Honor of Jacob M. Myers*. Edited by H. N. Bream et al. Gettysburg Theological Studies, 4. Philadelphia: Temple University Press, 1974.

> "The recognition of chiasmus in Job proves valuable in reducing the number of options in equivocal texts" (p. 128).

395 E. C. Webster. "Strophic Patterns in Job 3–28." *JSOT* 26 (1983): 33–60.

> "The basic period in the poetry of Job is the bicolon or tricolon . . . which are grouped into verse clusters or strophes" (p. 57).

396 P. van der Lugt. *Rhetorical Criticism and the Poetry of the Book of Job*. Oudtestamentische Studiën, 32. Leiden: E. J. Brill, 1995.

> History of investigation into the strophic structure of Job. Detailed analysis of the poetic structure of the three speech-cycles and the Elihu speech. Concluding observations on the

nature of biblical poetry. See also pp. 235–93 in *The Structural Analysis of Biblical and Canaanite Poetry* (#548).

397   S. B. Noegel. *Janus Parallelism in the Book of Job.* JSOTSup 223. Sheffield: Sheffield Academic, 1996.

Janus parallelism, "in which a middle stich of poetry parallels in a polysemous manner both the line that precedes it and the line that follows it" (p. 12), is "fundamental to the book's message" (p. 131).

3.5. Job as Literature

Perhaps more than any other biblical book, and not surprisingly, Job has been read solely for its dramatic and literary content (e.g., drama, comedy).

398   A. Cook. *The Root of the Thing: A Study of Job and the Song of Songs.* Bloomington: Indiana University Press, 1968.

Discussion of the dramatic form of these texts (e.g., drama, frame, parallelism, scene).

399   J. G. Williams. "'You Have Not Spoken Truth to Me': Mystery and Irony in Job." *ZAW* 83 (1971): 231–55.

"The poet does not take the epilogue to the Book of Job seriously, except insofar as it enhances the irony of the dialogue and theophany" (p. 250).

400   D. Robertson. "The Book of Job: A Literary Study." *Soundings* 56 (1973): 446–69.

Chapter-by-chapter analysis of Job's literary devices. Irony pervades the entire book. See also the response by E. M. Good (*Soundings* 56 [1973]: 470–84).

401   L. Alonso Schökel. "Toward a Dramatic Reading of the Book of Job." *Semeia* 7 (1977): 45–61.

Investigates interrelated concepts of ignorance, irony, and commitment on the part of Job's characters and the concept of God's justice. See response by J. Crenshaw (*Semeia* 7 [1977]: 63–39).

402   J. W. Whedbee. "The Comedy of Job." Pp. 1–39 in *Studies in the Book of Job.* Edited by R. Polzin and D. Robertson. Semeia, 7. Missoula: Scholars, 1977. Reprinted in *On Humour and the Comic in the Hebrew Bible.* JSOTSup 92. Bible and Literature

Series, 23. Edited by Y. T. Radday and A. Brenner. Sheffield: JSOT, 1990, pp. 217–49.

Working from the final form of the text, the author argues that Job belongs to the comedy genre, that is, the ironic, ludicrous, and ridiculous, which leads ultimately to the happiness of the hero. See response by D. Robertson (*Semeia* 7 [1977]: 41–44).

403 D. Penchansky. *The Betrayal of God: Ideological Conflict in Job.* Louisville: Westminster/John Knox, 1990.

Literary approach to Job that respects the "text as a site of conflict. It is the juncture of forces that impinge upon the act of reading, and each of these forces is a source of disharmonic elements that resist sense, resist aggressive interpretation" (p. 19).

404 J. B. Curtis. "Word Play in the Speeches of Elihu (Job 32–37)." *Proceedings, Eastern Great Lakes Biblical Society* 12 (1992): 23–30.

By the use of a number of literary devices, the writer of the Elihu speeches shows himself to be a sophisticated writer.

405 R. C. Schlobin. "Prototypic Horror: The Genre of the Book of Job." *Semeia* 60 (1992): 23–38.

Job is an example of the "horror genre" in that there is no certainty with God and he always transcends human understanding.

406 M. Cheney. *Dust, Wind and Agony: Character, Speech and Genre in Job.* Coniectanea Biblica Old Testament Series, 36. Stockholm: Almqvist & Wiksell, 1994.

Job in light of both ancient literature and modern literary analysis. Focuses on "one aspect of the book of Job, namely, character portrayal as it relates to genre and recorded speech" (p. 1).

3.6. Other

407 R. Laurin. "The Theological Structure of Job." *ZAW* 84 (1972): 86–89.

Chapter 28 of Job indicates that, for Job, "faith finds its basic ground only in a personal encounter with God" (p. 88).

408 G. Fohrer. "The Righteous Man in Job 31." Pp. 1–22 in *Essays in Old Testament Ethics: J. Philip Hyatt, In Memoriam*. Edited by J. L. Crenshaw. New York: KTAV, 1974.

Job's oath of purity in chapter 31 "describes the man who considers himself to be righteous before God . . . [who] therefore must be rebuked by God" (42:2–5; 42:2–3, 5–6) (p. 21).

409 J. H. Kahn. *Job's Illness: Loss, Grief and Integration: A Psychological Interpretation* Oxford/New York: Pergamon, 1975.

Job as "an illustration of basic human problems which patients describe when being treated for psychiatric disorders" (p. x).

410 C. P. Gavaler. "The Transformation of Job." *TBT* 30 (1992): 208–12.

Job learns from his ordeals that unconditional love is possible.

411 K. Nielsen. "Whatever Became of You, Satan? or a Literary-Critical Analysis of the Role of Satan in the Book of Job." Pp. 129–34 in *Goldene Äpfel in silbernen Schalen*. Beiträge zur Erforchung des alten Testament und des antiken Judentums, 20. Edited by K. D. Schunck and M. Augustin. Frankfurt am Main: Peter Lang, 1992.

Job and the Jacob narrative are analogous: father (God/Isaac) favors son (Job/Jacob) over jealous brother (Satan/Esau).

412 G. V. Smith. "Is There a Place for Job's Wisdom in Old Testament Theology?" *Trinity Journal* 13 (1992): 3–20.

"The sovereign God rules" is the message of Job as well as that of Torah and Prophets.

413 D. Bergant. "The Integrity of All Creation." *TBT* 33 (1995): 5–8.

Nature in Job provides revelatory content by which to know God.

4. Proverbs

Not unlike Psalms, Proverbs has generated a fair degree of scholarly activity that is focused on specific words, verses, or passages. Indeed, the structure of Proverbs itself seems to invite such an atomistic approach. It goes without saying that most of these studies cannot be included here. Some, however, that have an appeal beyond the boundaries of the specific verses in question have been included, but even here selectivity has been the rule. Also, both the wisdom (especially §1.1) and poetry sections should be consulted, as there is invariable overlap.

4.1. Introductions and Anthologies

414 R. E. Murphy. "The Faces of Wisdom in Proverbs." Pp. 336–45 in *Mélanges bibliques et orientaux en l'honneur de M. Henri Cazelles*. Alter Orient und Altes Testament, 212. Edited by A. Caquot and M. Delcor. Neukirchener Verlag, 1981.
Introduction to the variety of types of wisdom found in Proverbs: contrasts between chapters 1–9 and 10–31; wisdom as divine summons; wisdom as human response. Also includes discussion of the collections of units in Proverbs.

415 W. E. Mouser Jr. *Walking in Wisdom: Studying the Proverbs of Solomon*. Downers Grove: InterVarsity, 1983.
Popular introduction to the various poetic devices employed by the authors of Proverbs.

416 G. Van Rongen. *Be Wise! An Introduction to the Book of Proverbs.* Kelmscott, Western Australia: Pro Ecclesia, 1988.
Popular, broad introduction to the book as a whole and its themes.

417 J. J. Burden. "The Wisdom of Many: Recent Changes in Old Testament Proverb Interpretation." *Old Testament Essays* 3 (1990): 341–59.
"Investigates traditional, structural, contextual and linguistic approaches to paroemiology, the science of proverbs. The origin, nature, life setting, and function of the folk or traditional sayings are discussed" (p. 341).

418 C. R. Fontaine. "Wisdom in Proverbs." Pp. 99–114 in *In Search of Wisdom: Essays in Memory of John G. Gammie.* Edited by L. G. Perdue et al. Louisville: Westminster/John Knox, 1993.
Overview of the various social settings of Proverbs, its genre, and its presentation of wisdom.

419 R. E. Murphy. "Recent Research on Proverbs and Qoheleth." *Currents in Research: Biblical Studies* 1 (1993): 119–40.
Overview of basic issues in recent research. Includes bibliography.

420 R. C. Van Leeuwen. "Proverbs." Pp. 256–67 in *A Complete Literary Guide to the Bible.* Edited by L. Ryken and T. Longman III. Grand Rapids: Zondervan, 1993.
Proverbs is a coherent literary unit that is greater than the sum of its parts.

421 G. W. Parsons. "Guidelines for Understanding and Proclaiming the Book of Proverbs." *BSac* 150 (1993): 151–70. Reprinted in R. B. Zuck's *Learning from the Sages: Selected Studies on the Book of Proverbs.* Grand Rapids: Baker, 1995, pp. 151–68.
Five guidelines for understanding and proclaiming Proverbs are: (1) interpret passages in light of the whole book, (2) be sensitive to literary devices, (3) proverbs are not always unconditional, (4) some proverbs are unconditionally true, and (5) interpret Proverbs in light of ANE wisdom literature.

422 R. J. Clifford. *The Book of Proverbs and Our Search for Wisdom.* Milwaukee: Marquette University Press, 1995.
Brief introduction to Proverbs focusing on "(1) chapters 1–9 as a re-imagining of the moral life; (2) chapters 10–31 as a school of discernment; (3) the New Testament rereading" (p. 9).

423 J. D. Martin. *Proverbs*. Old Testament Guides. Sheffield: Sheffield Academic, 1995.

Introduction to the following topics in Proverbs scholarship: ANE context; Proverbs 1–9; Proverbs 10:1–29:27 ("Two 'Solomonic' Collections of Proverbs"); Proverbs 22:17–31:31 ("Appendices to the 'Solomonic' Collections"); Feminine in Proverbs; Wisdom and Theology.

424 W. S. Towner. "Proverbs and Its Successors." Pp. 157–75 in *Old Testament Interpretation: Past Present and Future*. Edited by J. L. Mays, D. L. Peterson, and K. H. Richards. Nashville: Abingdon, 1995.

Origins of proverbs; purpose of the book of Proverbs; topics addressed in Proverbs. Includes brief discussions of Ecclesiasticus and Wisdom of Solomon.

425 R. N. Whybray. *The Book of Proverbs: A Survey of Modern Study*. History of Biblical Interpretation Series, 1. Leiden: E. J. Brill, 1995.

Overview of Proverbs research in seven areas: Origins and Backgrounds; Proverbs 10–29; Proverbs 1–9 and 22:17–24:34; Proverbs 30–31; Ideas and Theology; Dating; Text and Versions.

426 R. B. Zuck (ed.). *Learning from the Sages: Selected Studies on the Book of Proverbs*. Grand Rapids: Baker, 1995.

Thirty-two previously published articles and essays on a wide variety of topics. The first ten deal with introductory matters while the remaining essays treat individual passages.

4.2. Original Setting, Development, and ANE Influence

Much of Proverbs scholarship is taken up with two broad themes: (1) the original Israelite setting in which these maxims arose and (2) the development of this early Israelite wisdom into the theological treatise we call the book of Proverbs. Some have posited a school setting for parts of the book. Others consider portions to have been used as instruction manuals for future rulers (a variation on the school hypothesis). The content of these proverbs is routinely seen to be connected with ANE wisdom traditions, particularly in light of the international and almost "secular" tone (which itself is a highly debated point; see #463). The book of Proverbs, however, does seem to represent the final stage of growth from a collection of originally independent units (either individual maxims or larger units). Some have argued that this collection also represents a process whereby these originally universal (i.e., non-Israelite) maxims were brought into conformity with orthodox Yahwism.

427 C. I. K. Story. "The Book of Proverbs and Northwest Semitic Literature." *JBL* 64 (1945): 319–37.

Ugaritic and Ahiqar compared to Proverbs. Ugaritic has clearly influenced Proverbs on the literary level, although the two are very different from a religious point of view. Ahiqar and Proverbs both stem from an older "romance" that personified wisdom, but the pagan connotations are missing in Proverbs.

428 P. Skehan. "A Single Editor for the Whole Book of Proverbs." *CBQ* 10 (1948): 115–30. Reprinted in Skehan's *Studies in Israelite Poetry and Wisdom*. CBQMS, 1. Washington, D.C.: Catholic Biblical Association of America, pp. 15–26, and in J. L. Crenshaw's *Studies in Ancient Israelite Wisdom*. New York: KTAV, 1976, pp. 329–40.

Argues that the postexilic author of Proverbs 1–9 was the "sole editor for substantially all of the Book" (p. 329).

429 R. N. Whybray. "Proverbs VIII 22–31 and Its Supposed Prototypes." *VT* 15 (1965): 504–14. Reprinted in J. L. Crenshaw's *Studies in Ancient Israelite Wisdom*. New York: KTAV, 1976, pp. 390–400.

Compares Proverbs 8:22–31 with Genesis 1:1–3, 2:4b–7, and Egyptian and Babylonian creation accounts. Concludes that these texts are not truly comparable, their only similarity stemming from common subject matter and the use of negative temporal clauses. Doubts the value of speaking of a common tradition or prototype behind the various accounts.

430 M. V. Fox. "Aspects of the Religion of the Book of Proverbs." *HUCA* 39 (1968): 55–69.

Proverbs has gone through three stages in its historical development: Egyptian origins, harmonization (albeit incomplete) of Egyptian wisdom and normative Yahwism, and a more thorough theological outworking of this synthesis. The dates of these three stages cannot be determined absolutely, only relatively, although the final stage probably stems from either the Persian or Hellenistic period. The type of wisdom exemplified by Proverbs is not speculative but ethical-religious, that is, functional, the purpose of which is "to get people to behave morally" (p. 55).

431 R. B. Y. Scott. "Wise and Foolish, Righteous and Wicked." Pp. 146–65 in *Studies in the Religion of Ancient Israel*. VTSup 23. Leiden: E. J. Brill, 1972.

Proverbs is the end product of a long history of collection, supplementing, and editing. Seven types of sayings are posited, three of religious content and four of secular content.

432 B. W. Kovacs. "Is There a Class-Ethic in Proverbs?" Pp. 171–89 in *Essays in Old Testament Ethics: J. Philip Hyatt, In Memoriam*. Edited by J. L. Crenshaw and J. T. Willis. New York: KTAV, 1974.

The title's question is answered in the affirmative: the sages "possessed a distinctive value-system which revalued the life and behavior of outsiders to such a degree that we regard it as an in-group morality, though by no means closed to the world" (p. 187).

433 J. M. Thompson. *The Form and Function of Proverbs in Ancient Israel*. The Hague and Paris: Mouton, 1974.

Defense of the writer's conviction that Proverbs "deserves both its place within the Canon and the high regard which it formerly received" (p. 8). An examination of the form and function of proverbs in general, in the ANE, and in Israel shows that their form is poetic and their function is philosophical (to instruct, entertain, and preserve legal tradition). Proverbs later influenced Israel's prophetic and priestly traditions.

434 H. J. Postel. "The Form and Function of the Motive Clause in Proverbs 10–29." Ph.D. dissertation, University of Iowa, 1976.

Technical study that argues, among other things, that "those sections of Proverbs with the highest percentage of motive clauses also [offer] the greatest degree of correspondences with Egyptian wisdom literature, and especially with reference to the Instruction genre" (p. 179).

435 J. Ruffle. "The Teaching of Amenemope and Its Connection with the Book of Proverbs." *TB* 28 (1977): 29–68. Reprinted in R. B. Zuck's *Learning from the Sages: Selected Studies on the Book of Proverbs*. Grand Rapids: Baker, 1995, pp. 293–331.

There is no support for the claim that the authors of Proverbs borrowed their material from *The Teaching of Amenemope*. Similarities are mainly on the level of subject matter, but the two treat these subjects differently.

436 W. L. Humphreys. "The Motif of the Wise Courtier in the Book of Psalms." Pp. 177–90 in *Israelite Wisdom: Theological and Literary Essays in Honor of Samuel Terrien*. Edited by J. G. Gammie et al. Missoula: Scholars, 1978.

Compares Proverbs 10–29 with Egyptian wisdom texts to investigate the prevailing scholarly notion that the *locus classicus* for biblical wisdom was its didactic role in the royal court. Proverbs 10–29 did not serve as a "core curriculum in the training of future courtiers" (p. 178).

437 B. K. Waltke. "The Book of Proverbs and Ancient Wisdom Literature." *BSac* 136 (1979): 221–38. Reprinted in R. B. Zuck's *Learning from the Sages: Selected Studies on the Book of Proverbs.* Grand Rapids: Baker, 1995, pp. 49–65.

A preexilic date and Solomonic authorship are plausible for much of Proverbs. Wisdom denotes a fixed order to which the righteous man submits.

438 B. V. Malchow. "A Manual for Future Monarchs: Proverbs 27:23–29:27." *CBQ* 47 (1985): 238–45. Reprinted in R. B. Zuck's *Learning from the Sages: Selected Studies on the Book of Proverbs,* pp. 353–60. Grand Rapids: Baker, 1995.

This passage is a unified collection that functioned as a manual for future leaders in Israel.

439 N. Shupak. "The 'Sitz im Leben' of the Book of Proverbs in Light of a Comparison of Biblical and Egyptian Wisdom Literature." *RB* 94 (1987): 98–119.

There is evidence in Proverbs of schools, and "the first schools in Israel were inspired by an Egyptian prototype" (p. 98).

440 J. L. Crenshaw. "The Sage in Proverbs." Pp. 205–16 in *The Sage in Israel and the Ancient Near East.* Edited by J. G. Gammie and L. G. Perdue. Winona Lake, Ind.: Eisenbrauns, 1990.

Suggests three contexts for Israelite learning (family, school, court) and three formal settings of learning (pragmatic, secular, religious). Some discussion of the audiences of wisdom (the common people vis-à-vis the elite).

441 D. C. Snell. *Twice-Told Proverbs and the Composition of the Book of Proverbs.* Winona Lake, Ind.: Eisenbrauns, 1993.

Repetitions in the book of Proverbs hold the key to understanding the history of the book's composition.

442 J. L. Crenshaw. "Prohibitions in Proverbs and Qoheleth." Pp. 115–24 in *Priests, Prophets and Scribes: Essays on the Formation and Heritage of Second Temple Judaism in Honour of Joseph Blenkinsopp.* Edited by E. Ulrich, et al. JSOTSup 149. Sheffield: JSOT, 1992.

Analysis of the language of prohibitions in Proverbs and Qoheleth provides evidence that wisdom and law do not have a common origin.

443 R. N. Whybray. "Thoughts on the Composition of Proverbs 10–29." Pp. 102–24 in *Priests, Prophets and Scribes: Essays on the Formation and Heritage of Second Temple Judaism in Honour of Joseph Blenkinsopp*. Edited by E. Ulrich, et al. JSOTSup 149. Sheffield: JSOT, 1992.

Discusses four views on the lengthy process of compilation of Proverbs 10–29. An earlier or original collection of Proverbs was added to for a variety of possible reasons.

4.3. Structure

Some scholars have espoused the view that Proverbs is merely a loose (even random) collection of individual, isolated sayings. Such an extreme view has no doubt given others reason to search for evidence of structure and coherence throughout the book. It is now a commonly held position that Proverbs exhibits strong indications of purposeful design, both on the macro and micro levels.

444 P. Skehan. "Wisdom's House." *CBQ* 29 (1967): 162–80. Reprinted in Skehan's *Studies in Israelite Poetry and Wisdom*. CBQMS, 1. Washington, D.C.: Catholic Biblical Association, 1971, pp. 27–45.

Argues that the author of Proverbs ruled his manuscript (a total of three with fifteen lines). Although each column could hold twenty-five lines of text, only the middle section (10:1–22:16) actually held that many. The total picture gives the appearance of a tripartite, houselike structure.

445 W. McKane. "Functions of Language and Objectives of Discourse according to Proverbs 10–30." Pp. 166–85 in *La Sagesse de l'Ancien Testament*. Edited by M. Gilbert. BETL, 51. Leuven: Leuven University Press, 1979.

Proverbs "[makes] a point elegantly and [combines] brevity with a well-finished appearance" (p. 167). Brevity in communication is a function of the sages' awareness of the misuses of language.

446 R. N. Whybray. "Yahweh-sayings and Their Contexts in Proverbs 10,1—22,16." Pp. 153–65 in *La Sagesse de l'Ancien Testament*. Edited by M. Gilbert. BETL, 51. Leuven: Leuven University Press, 1979.

Proverbs is a purposeful collection of sayings that betray redactional design. Sayings are grouped in pairs or larger groups. Yahweh-sayings are juxtaposed to older secular sayings in an effort to "assert the absolute primacy of Yahweh" (p. 165).

447 J. G. Williams. "The Power of Form: A Study of Biblical Proverbs." *Semeia* 17 (1980): 35–58. Reprinted in R. B. Zuck's *Learning from the Sages: Selected Studies on the Book of Proverbs*. Grand Rapids: Baker, 1995, pp. 73–97.

"There are definite artistic forms and methods in the sentence literature of the book of Proverbs. Recognizing these forms and methods may contribute to a renewed literary and religious appreciation of the proverbs" (p. 35).

448 T. Hildebrandt. "Proverbial Pairs: Compositional Units in Proverbs 10–29." *JBL* 107 (1988): 201–24.

Proverbs should be read atomistically. The "proverbial pair" is "a discrete level of composition" (p. 218), which is an indication of editorial purpose.

449 T. A. Perry. *Wisdom Literature and the Structure of Proverbs*. University Park: Pennsylvania State University Press, 1993.

Application of a "quadripartite" grid to proverbial sayings, which brings to the surface concealed structures.

450 R. N. Whybray. *The Composition of the Book of Proverbs*. JSOTSup 168. Sheffield: JSOT, 1994.

Proverbs 1–9 and 31:10–31 provide the framework for the book. Within this frame are found other collections of proverbs (e.g., headings on 10:1 and 22:17).

4.4. Proverbs 1–9

Of all the sections in Proverbs, chapters 1–9 have attracted a disproportionate amount of attention. As the opening section of the book, it is thought to hold keys to how the book as a whole is to be understood. There is some debate whether these chapters represent the final stage in the editing of the book (postexilic) or whether they are consistent with a monarchic or even Solomonic setting. The personification of Lady Wisdom in chapter 8 is essentially unique in the OT, although it has a number of parallels in the ANE and postbiblical Jewish literature (Sira 24, Wisdom 10).

451 P. Skehan. "The Seven Columns of Wisdom's House in Proverbs 1–9." *CBQ* 9 (1947): 190–98. Reprinted in Skehan's *Studies in*

Israelite Poetry and Wisdom. CBQMS, 1. Washington, D.C.: Catholic Biblical Association, 1971, pp. 9–14.

The "seven columns" mentioned in Proverbs 9:1 are the "seven poems of uniform length which extend through chaps. 2–7 inclusive" (p. 9).

452 R. N. Whybray. *Wisdom in Proverbs: The Concept of Wisdom in Proverbs 1–9.* Studies in Biblical Theology, 45. London: SCM/Naperville, Ill.: Allenson, 1965.

"These chapters are not a literary unity expressing a single concept of wisdom, but consist of an original lesson-book designed for use in scribal schools and closely modelled on Egyptian prototypes, to which later writers have added interpretive material with the intention of bringing its teaching more closely into conformity with Israelite religious beliefs" (p. 7).

453 R. Tournay. "Proverbs 1–9: A First Theological Synthesis of the Tradition of the Sages." Pp. 51–61 in *The Dynamism of Biblical Tradition (Concilium 20).* New York, 1967.

Proverbs 1–9 is an apologia for traditional Yahwism. The sage "exploits the ancient scriptures by transposing them into a new perspective, that of creation" (p. 61).

454 B. L. Mack. "Wisdom Myth and Mytho-logy: An Essay in Understanding a Theological Tradition." *Int* 24 (1970): 46–60.

Proverbs 1–9, by employing the mytho-logical imagery of personified wisdom, is one example of an exilic attempt to explain Yahweh's lordship over all of creation in light of Israel's national tragedy. The exile does not require resignation but faith, for wisdom is a constant element in creation.

455 N. C. Habel. "The Symbolism of Wisdom in Proverbs 1–9." *Int* 26 (1972): 131–57.

"The way" in Proverbs is "a basic nuclear expression" that "has a system of satellite symbols or images" (p. 133) (personal human experience, Yahwistic religion, cosmological reflection).

456 M. O. Gilchrist. "Proverbs 1–9: Instruction or Riddle?" *Proceedings, Eastern Great Lakes Biblical Society* 4 (1984): 131–45.

Proverbs is not simply instruction. The variety of imagery used in chapters 1–9 to portray wisdom points toward "complexity and ambiguity in the quest for wisdom" (p. 131).

457 R. E. Murphy. "Wisdom and Eros in Proverbs 1–9." *CBQ* 50 (1988): 600–603.

> "Sexual fidelity is also a symbol of one's attachment to Lady Wisdom" (p. 603).

458 R. C. Van Leeuwen. "Liminality and Worldview in Proverbs 1–9." *Semeia* 50 (1990): 111–44.

> The "root metaphors" of chapters 1–9 are found in the "larger metaphoric system and polarity of Wisdom/Folly, Good/Pseudo Good, Life/Death" (p. 111). Contends directly with both Camp (#472) and Habel (#455).

459 S. L. Harris. *Proverbs 1–9: A Study of Inner-Biblical Interpretation.* SBLDS, 150. Atlanta: Scholars, 1996.

> Proverbs employs the Joseph story and Jeremiah, and, hence, is not devoid of interaction with Israel's historical literature.

4.5. Theology/Teaching

It is not an exercise in reductionism to say that Proverbs focuses on moral content. Of any book in the OT it can be said of Proverbs that its purpose is to guide its readers in standards of conduct. In addition to the teachings of the individual maxims, the theology of larger sections and of Proverbs as a whole have garnered their share of attention. What does the book say about God? Another issue that has attracted attention recently is the notion of the feminine in Proverbs, an issue that stems from the identification of wisdom as a woman in chapter 8. Also a number of works have appeared concerning wealth in Proverbs.

4.5.1. General

460 R. E. Murphy. "The Kerygma of the Book of Proverbs." *Int* 20 (1966): 3–14.

> Despite its clear international flavor and the absence of *Heilsgeschichte*, Proverbs does evince a kerygmatic nature, which can be summed up in one word: life (8:32–36).

461 H. Blocher. "The Fear of the Lord Is the 'Principle' of Wisdom." *TynBul* 28 (1977): 3–28.

> The famous maxim of Proverbs 1:7 ("The fear of the LORD is the *beginning* of wisdom") means that wisdom has a religious foundation: true knowledge must "[proceed] in the knowledge of God, and [acknowledge] his absolute lordship" (p. 17).

462 B. Vawter. "Prov. 8:22: Wisdom and Creation." *JBL* 99 (1980): 205–16.

In Job 28 and Proverbs 8:22, wisdom is "neither God's creation nor his natural attribute but rather a possession which he (unlike man) has acquired" (p. 205). The root *qnh* does not refer to the creation of wisdom but to divine acquisition.

463 B. K. Waltke. "The Authority of Proverbs: An Exposition of Proverbs 1:2–6." *Presbyterion* 13 (1987): 65–78.

The book of Proverbs is not simply human advice but claims to be divinely authoritative. "Wisdom" is synonymous with "law," "commandment," and "fear of the Lord." See also Waltke's "Lady Wisdom as Mediatrix: An Exposition of Proverbs 1:20–33." *Presbyterion* 14 (1988): 1–15. Reprinted in R. B. Zuck's *Learning from the Sages: Selected Studies on the Book of Proverbs.* Grand Rapids: Baker, 1995, pp. 191–204.

464 F. M. Wilson. "Sacred and Profane? The Yahwistic Redaction of Proverbs Reconsidered." Pp. 313–34 in *The Listening Heart: Essays in Wisdom and the Psalms in Honor of Roland E. Murphy, O. Carm.* Edited by K. G. Hoglund et al. JSOTSup 58. Sheffield: JSOT, 1987.

Analysis of previous attempts to explain the "problem" of the presence of sacred and profane wisdom in Proverbs. Concludes that mundane wisdom is not interpreted Yahwistically to give it theological significance. Rather, there is a "complementary and reciprocal" relationship between theological and mundane wisdom (p. 328).

465 L. E. Toombs. "The Theology and Ethics of the Book of Proverbs." *Consensus* 14, no. 2 (1988): 7–24.

"Proverbs provides a model of the way in which theology and secular life may be brought into constructive contact without undermining the theological foundation or playing down the significance of rational thought or secular experience" (p. 7).

466 L. Boström. *The God of the Sages: The Portrayal of God in the Book of Proverbs.* Coniectanea Biblica. Old Testament Series, 29. Stockholm: Almqvist & Wiksell, 1990.

Israelite wisdom as reflected in Proverbs, although expressing an international outlook and emphasizing themes that are not as developed in the historical books (creation, justice/ethics), is nevertheless complementary to salvation history.

467 R. E. Clements. "The Good Neighbor in the Book of Proverbs." Pp. 209–28 in *Of Prophets' Visions and the Wisdom of the Sages: Essays in Honour of R. Norman Whybray on His Seventieth Birthday*. Edited by H. A. McKay and D. J. A. Clines. JSOTSup 162. Sheffield: JSOT, 1993.

Proverbs' teaching on one's relationship to one's neighbor falls under three general categories: neighbor in need, wealth, talkativeness.

468 J. Mulrooney. "Wisdom to Live By." *TBT* 31 (1993): 272–76.

Life is full of choices and Proverbs puts before the reader the choice between wisdom and folly.

4.5.2. Feminine

469 C. V. Camp. *Wisdom and the Feminine in the Book of Proverbs*. Bible and Literature Series, 11. Sheffield: Almond, 1985.

The metaphor of "Woman Wisdom" serves as a literary metaphor to bring under one heading the feminine in wisdom. Six female types are identified: wife, lover, harlot/adulteress, wise woman, woman who uses indirect means to effect God's ends, woman who authenticates written tradition. See also Camp's essay in *The Bible and the Politics of Exegesis* (ed. D. Jobling, P. L. Day, and G. T. Sheppard [Cleveland: Pilgrim, 1991]), pp. 17–31.

470 T. P. McCreesh. "Wisdom as Wife: Proverbs 31:10–31." *RB* 92 (1985): 25–46. Reprinted in R. B. Zuck's *Learning from the Sages: Selected Studies on the Book of Proverbs*. Grand Rapids: Baker, 1995, pp. 391–410.

The picture of the faithful and skillful wife of Proverbs 31 presents a picture of wisdom. She is not remote but a practical and ever-present guide.

471 B. Lang. *Wisdom and the Book of Proverbs: An Israelite Goddess Redefined*. New York: Pilgrim, 1986.

Analysis of three coherent poems in Proverbs (1:20–33; chap. 8, chap. 9) that have been "overlaid with a veneer of mono-Yahwism" (p. 6) obscuring goddess Wisdom, but still provide glimpses into the original.

472 C. V. Camp. "Woman Wisdom as Root Metaphor: A Theological Consideration." Pp. 45–76 in *The Listening Heart: Essays in Wisdom and the Psalms in Honor of Roland E. Murphy, O. Carm.* Edited by K. G. Hoglund et al. JSOTSup 58. Sheffield: JSOT, 1987.

Building on her previous work (#469), Camp explores to what extent "Woman Wisdom" "can function as an authoritative image for theology, and especially for feminist theology" (p. 47).

473 C. V. Camp. "Wise and Strange: An Interpretation of the Female Imagery in Proverbs in Light of Trickster Mythology." *Semeia* 42 (1988): 14–36.

Reading the female figures in Proverbs in light of the trickster figure from comparative myth and folklore "has the effect of undercutting the book's most obvious message of absolute opposition between good and evil as represented in the female figures, and highlighting their paradoxical, but experientially validated, unity" (p. 14).

474 A. Brenner. "Proverbs 1–9: An F Voice?" Pp. 113–30 in *On Gendering Texts: Female and Male Voices in the Hebrew Bible.* Edited by A. Brenner and F. Van Dijk-Hemmes. Leiden: E. J. Brill, 1993.

Proverbs 1–9 can be read as a mother's encouragement to her sons to obey their father. In doing so, she would have internalized the oppressor's androcentrism.

4.5.3. Wealth

475 R. N. Whybray. *Wealth and Poverty in the Book of Proverbs.* JSOTSup 99. Sheffield: Sheffield Academic, 1990.

Proverbs displays differing viewpoints on the subject of wealth and poverty, but remains "on the whole uncritical of the *status quo*" (p. 10).

476 R. L. Giese Jr. "Qualifying Wealth in the Septuagint of Proverbs." *JBL* 111 (1992): 409–25.

LXX Proverbs is even more concerned than Hebrew Proverbs to demonstrate that wealth is a reward for those who pursue wisdom.

477 R. C. Van Leeuwen. "Wealth and Poverty: System and Contradiction in Proverbs." *Hebrew Studies* 33 (1992): 25–36.

The sages recognize the inequities of life: the righteous do not always prosper and the wicked are not always poor. Job and Qoheleth do not contradict Proverbs but expound further on this theme.

478 H. C. Washington. *Wealth and Poverty in the Instruction of Amenemope and the Hebrew Proverbs.* SBLDS 142. Atlanta: Scholars, 1994.

Comparison of the historical setting that forms the background of *The Instructions of Amenemope* and Proverbs 22:17–24:22. The biblical defense of the poor is evidence of influence of this Egyptian work.

4.6. Other

479 D. W. Thomas. "Textual and Philological Notes on Some Passages in the Book of Proverbs." Pp. 280–92 in *Wisdom in Israel and in the Ancient Near East: Presented to Professor Harold Henry Rowley.* Edited by M. Noth and D. W. Thomas. VTSup 3. Leiden: E. J. Brill, 1955.

Comments on seventeen problematic passages in Proverbs: 1:4; 1:11; 1:17; 3:35; 6:26; 7:21; 10:32; 14:8; 14:17; 15:30; 19:17; 19:18; 19:26; 22:4; 30:16; 30:31; 31:11.

480 B. W. Kovacs. "Sociological-Structural Constraints upon Wisdom: The Spatial and Temporal Matrix of Proverbs 15:28–22:16." Ph.D. dissertation, Vanderbilt, 1978.

A social-historical analysis of Proverbs 15:28–22:16 "can help us refine our understanding of this literature and its social, historical, literary and theological character" (p. 13).

481 J. J. Collins. "Proverbial Wisdom and the Yahwist Vision." *Semeia* 17 (1980): 1–17.

Even though the Yahwist vision is characterized by prophecy and parables, both the Yahwist vision and proverbial wisdom affirm "a sense of the historical transience of human existence which exposes the limitations of all human knowledge" (p. 1).

482 P. J. Nel. *The Structure and Ethos of the Wisdom Admonitions in Proverbs.* BZAW, 158. Berlin: de Gruyter, 1982.

"The ethos of the wisdom [admonition?] can be described successfully, provided that the function and role of the motivation is duly considered and that the inner logic of the coherence admonition-motivation is grasped" (p. 126). (See #171.)

483 E. Huwiler. "Control of Reality in Israelite Wisdom." Ph.D. dissertation, Duke University, 1988.

Application of reader–response criticism to the sentence wisdom in Proverbs. Challenges the assumed "adequacy of the developmental schemes of Israelite wisdom which depend on the independence of individual sentences" (p. 242). The sages' relationship to reality was as complex and varied as that reality itself.

484 T. P. McCreesh. *Biblical Sound Sense: Poetic Sound Patterns in Proverbs 10–29.* JSOTSup 128. Sheffield: JSOT, 1991.

Sound patterns (assonance and rhyme) are of crucial importance for understanding Proverbs. They are used "to please the ear, to attract attention, to make speech worth remembering, to indicate contrast or agreement, and the like" (p. 155).

Part 2

5. Poetry

The following items deal with biblical poetry. Poetry is not restricted to the Psalms. It is also found in the wisdom literature, Song of Songs, and Lamentations, and is interspersed throughout narrative portions of the OT as well. The topics that are discussed under this rubric are broad and far-reaching. In addition to general introductions, several works treat the history of scholarship and assess recent trends. More focused studies are often devoted to such perennial issues as the nature of poetic parallelism, meter, chiasm and other structural devices, numerical sayings, ANE influence (especially Ugaritic), and poetry in narrative contexts. As even a brief investigation will show, it is virtually impossible to keep these topics separate. In view of the amount of overlap between them, it seems best not to impose rigid categories. Therefore, the material is presented below in chronological order.

5.1. Before 1960

485 L. I. Newman and W. Popper. *Studies in Biblical Parallelism*. Berkeley: University of California Press, 1918.
> Thorough examination of poetic parallelism in Amos and Isaiah with a view toward solving problems where the parallelism

seems defective. Includes lengthy introduction to the origin
and development of parallelism, particularly in the ANE and
postbiblical times.

486 T. H. Robinson. "Anacrusis in Hebrew Poetry." Pp. 37–40 in *Werden und Wesen des Alten Testaments*. Edited by P. Volz et al. BZAW, 66. Berlin: A. Töpelmann, 1936.

Assuming the occasional presence of anacrusis (an unstressed syllable at the beginning of the line) will help make sense of a poetic line's metrical structure without resorting to emendations.

487 C. F. Kraft. *The Strophic Structure of Hebrew Poetry as Illustrated in the First Book of the Psalter.* Chicago: University of Chicago Press, 1938.

Includes history of past and recent scholarship on strophic studies. The strophic composition of Psalms 1–41 is remarkably consistent, with the couplet and triad predominating (also quatrains and the occasional addition of half lines).

488 W. O. E. Oesterley. *Ancient Hebrew Poems: Metrically Translated with Introductions and Notes.* New York: Macmillan, 1938.

Semipopular translation of twenty-nine biblical and three apocryphal poems that attempts to "reproduce the Hebrew rhythmic beats" (p. 7). Includes textual notes at the end of each translation.

489 J. A. Montgomery. "Stanza Formation in Hebrew Poetry." *JBL* 64 (1945): 379–84.

Focuses on the Psalms and concludes "there was some inner urge in Hebrew poetry, however unconscious, towards balance and proportion" (p. 381).

490 T. H. Robinson. *The Poetry of the Old Testament.* London: Duckworth, 1947.

Discusses the characteristics of biblical poetry. Most of the book interacts directly with the various biblical poetical books. Includes helpful annotated bibliography compiled by A. Johnson.

491 J. Muilenburg. "A Study in Hebrew Rhetoric: Repetition and Style." Pp. 97–111 in *Congress Volume: Copenhagen, 1953.* VTSup 1. Leiden: E. J. Brill, 1953.

Survey of the phenomenon of repetition (i.e., "parallel" lines) in the OT "as a major feature of Hebrew rhetoric and style" (p. 99).

492 T. H. Robinson. "Hebrew Poetic Form: The English Tradition."
Pp. 128–49 in *Congress Volume: Copenhagen, 1953*. VTSup 1.
Leiden: E. J. Brill, 1953.

Scholarship on biblical parallelism from the time of Lowth's
ground-breaking work, *De Sacra Poesi Hebraeorum*.

493 P. P. Saydon. "Assonance in Hebrew as a Means of Expressing
Emphasis." *Bib* 36 (1955): 36–50, 287–304.

Provides many examples, mainly from the Prophets, for the
use of assonance for emphasis in biblical poetry. Some assonance, however, is merely aesthetic rather than emphatic.

494 S. Mowinckel. *Real and Apparent Tricola in Hebrew Psalm
Poetry*. Oslo: Norske Videnskaps Akademi, 1957.

There are many cases in the OT "where an apparent tricolon
is only due to inaccurate textual transmission" (p. 100). A pre-
dominantly bicolic psalm will generally not contain isolated
tricola or isolated single cola.

5.2. 1960s

495 R. G. Boling. "'Synonymous' Parallelism in the Psalms." *JSS* 5
(1960): 221–55.

In the Psalter, "words are used in parallelism according to relatively fixed traditional sequences" (p. 223). Focuses on common word sequences and divine names in parallelism, and
includes numerous lists of word pairs.

496 D. N. Freedman. "Archaic Forms in Early Hebrew Poetry." *ZAW*
72 (1960): 101–7.

Meter in archaic Hebrew poetry served not merely an orna-
mental but a structural function. "Balance or symmetry is a
principal characteristic of early Hebrew poetic structure, deriv-
ing apparently from its musical framework" (p. 101).

497 S. Segert. "Problems of Hebrew Prosody." Pp. 283–91 in *Congress Volume: Oxford, 1959*. VTSup 7. Leiden: E. J. Brill, 1960.

Suggests problems in three theories of Hebrew prosody: (1) "the
identification of the word with the prosodical unit"; (2) "Hebrew
verse is formed by accuntuated [sic] feet"; (3) the "alternation
of stressed and unstressed syllables" (pp. 283–84).

498 E. Z. Melamad. "The Break-up of Stereotype Phrases as an Artistic Device in Biblical Poetry." Pp. 115–53 in *Studies in the Bible*.

Ed. C. Rabin. Scripta hierosolymitana, 8. Jerusalem: Magnes, 1961.

> Biblical poets "habitually break up compound linguistic stereotypes into their two components, placing one in the first half of the verse and the other in the second, with the result that the two halves become still more tightly interlocked" (p. 152).

499 S. Gevirtz. *Patterns in the Early Poetry of Israel*. Studies in Ancient Oriental Civilizations, 32. Chicago: University of Chicago Press, 1963.

> Studies of five older biblical poems (eulogy of Saul and David; Lamech's song; Isaac's blessing; Balaam's first mashal; David's lament over Saul and Jonathan). These early poets were heirs to a Syro-Palestinian poetic tradition that employed fixed pairs set in parallel structure. Parallelism is seen not so much on the level of meter but in the use of fixed word pairs.

500 H. Kosmala. "Form and Structure in Ancient Hebrew Poetry (A New Approach)." *VT* 14 (1964): 423–45 and 16 (1966): 152–80.

> Interacting mainly with Isaiah, examines criteria for determining what made up the original text of a poetic section. The basic element of ancient Hebrew poetry is "the word-or thought-unit irrespective of beats and stresses" (pp. 425–26). A poetic unit is anything "that can be expressed by one essential word" (p. 426).

501 M. Held. "The Action–Result (Factitive–Passive) Sequence of Identical Verbs in Biblical Hebrew and Ugaritic." *JBL* 84 (1965): 272–82.

> "In certain poetic verses of the Hebrew Bible which contain two hemistichs, we find the same verb used in both, with the second hemistich expressing the result of the action described in the first. This is accomplished by a change in stem, e.g., nifal-qal or stative-factitive" (p. 272).

502 W. M. W. Roth. *Numerical Sayings in the OT: A Form-Critical Study*. VTSup 13. Leiden: E. J. Brill, 1965.

> Examines use of the numerical saying in narrative, reflective, and hortative contexts. Widely used throughout the OT and serves basically a philosophic-didactic function

503 M. J. Dahood. "A New Metrical Pattern in Biblical Poetry." *CBQ* 29 (1967): 574–82.

The "double-duty modifier" yields a balanced metrical pattern between the two poetic lines it serves (e.g., 8:2:8).

504 S. E. Loewenstamm. "The Expanded Colon in Ugaritic and Biblical Verse." *JSS* 14 (1969): 176–96.

Investigation of formulas, typically addresses that intervene in parallel cola, such as, "God of vengeance, *O Lord*. / God of vengeance, shine forth" (Ps 104:1). The presence of this phenomenon is "more diversified and developed than in Ugaritic poetry" (p. 186).

5.3. 1970s

505 J. J. Glück. "Assonance in Ancient Hebrew Poetry: Sound Patterns as a Literary Device." Pp. 69–84 in *De Fructu Oris Sui: Essays in Honour of Adrianus Van Selms*. Edited by I. H. Eybers, F. C. Fensham, et al. Leiden: E. J. Brill, 1971.

Discusses poetry from a variety of OT books to demonstrate that assonance "stimulated the listener to receive his message as beautiful and believable" (p. 84).

506 P. B. Yoder. "A–B Pairs and Oral Composition in Hebrew Poetry." *VT* 21 (1971): 470–89.

Ugaritic and Hebrew poets seemed to rely on a stock of fixed word pairs (a "dictionary of parallel words" [p. 472]). Use of word pairs, although exhibiting great variety, argues for oral composition of poems.

507 Y. Avishur. "Pairs of Synonymous Words in the Construct State (and in Appositional Hendiadys) in Biblical Hebrew." *Semitics* 2 (1971–72): 17–81.

Survey of synonymous words in the construct state (provides 106 examples; 16 of appositional hendiadys). The semantic relationship between the two terms in the pair varies.

508 G. B. Gray. *The Forms of Hebrew Poetry*. Second Edition: New York: KTAV, 1972.

A classic volume whose point of departure is Lowth's seminal study *De Sacra Poesi Hebraeorum Praelectiones Academicae*. The essential characteristics of Hebrew poetry are parallelism and rhythm. Includes a prolegomenon and annotated bibliography by D. N. Freedman.

509   D. N. Freedman. "Acrostics and Metrics in Hebrew Poetry." *Harvard Theological Review* 65 (1972): 367–92. Reprinted in Freedman's *Pottery, Poetry, and Prophecy: Studies in Early Hebrew Poetry.* Winona Lake, Ind.: Eisenbrauns, 1980, pp. 51–76 (#532).
Focusing mainly on Lamentations, studies the metrical structure of acrostic poems. Most acrostic poems have lines averaging 16 1/2 syllables while Lamentations 1–4 averages 13 to 14 syllables. There is a fairly wide range of line length exhibited in the acrostics. The argument is expanded in Freedman's "Acrostic Poems in the Hebrew Bible: Alphabetic and Otherwise." *CBQ* 48 (1986): 408–31.

510   M. Haran. "The Graded Numerical Sequence and the Phenomenon of 'Automatism' in Biblical Poetry." Pp. 238–67 in *Congress Volume: Uppsala, 1971.* VTSup 22. Edited by H. Nyberg et al. Leiden: E. J. Brill, 1972.
The graded numerical phrase $(n + 1)$ can be broken up between two members of a parallel line. Special attention given to the presence of this phenomenon in Amos.

511   D. A. Robertson. *Linguistic Evidence in Dating Early Hebrew Poetry.* SBLDS, 3. Missoula: Scholars, 1972.
Analysis of biblical poetic portions considered early "to determine whether any biblical poetry can be dated to the early period of Israelite historical development" (p. ix), that is, thirteenth to tenth centuries B.C. Exodus 15 is the only unambiguously early biblical poem.

512   D. Broadribb. "A Historical Review of Studies of Hebrew Poetry." *Abr-Nahrain* 13 (1972–73): 66–87.
Reviews, "chronologically and thematically, the basic steps taken over the past centuries to formulate the nature of classical Hebrew poetry" (p. 66). There has been little significant advance over the past two or three centuries.

513   A. Baker. "Parallelism: England's Contribution to Biblical Studies." *CBQ* 35 (1973): 429–40.
Review of R. Lowth's contribution to the study of biblical poetry.

514   M. J. Dahood. "The Breakup of Stereotyped Phrases." *Journal of the Ancient Near Eastern Society of Columbia University* 5 (1973): 83–89.

Awareness of this phenomenon will help the exegete "to determine the sense of ambiguous expressions or to identify poetic
usages hitherto overlooked" (p. 83).

515 M. Z. Kaddari. "A Semantic Approach to Biblical Parallelism."
Journal of Jewish Studies 24 (1973): 167–75.
Explores the use of semantic parallelism by lexicographers to
determine meaning. Semantic parallelism cannot be assumed
in biblical poetry.

516 R. L. Alden. "Chiastic Psalms: A Study in the Mechanics of
Semitic Poetry in Psalms 1–50." *Journal of the Evangelical The-
ological Society* 17 (1974): 11–28. See *Journal of the Evangelical
Theological Society* 19 (1976): 191–200 for part II (Pss. 51–100).
Discussion of those psalms in Psalms 1–100 that are chiasti-
cally arranged.

517 J. H. Stek. "The Stylistics of Hebrew Poetry: A (Re)New(ed) Focus
of Study." *Calvin Theological Journal* 9 (1974): 15–30.
Call for appreciation of the artistry of OT poetry (alliteration,
chiasmus, parallelism). Proper interpretation of poetic texts
"demands full appreciation for and understanding of their *literary* quality" (p. 29).

518 Y. Avishur. "Word Pairs Common to Phoenician and Biblical
Hebrew." *Ugarit-Forschungen* 7 (1975): 13–47.
Lists, in context with comments, over forty word pairs that
Phoenician and biblical poetry share. Some of the common-
ality is not a result of any genetic relationship between the
two, whereas some pairs indicate direct borrowing of Phoenician pairs by Hebrew poets.

519 F. M. Cross Jr. and D. N. Freedman. *Studies in Ancient Yahwistic Poetry*. SBLDS, 21. Missoula: Scholars, 1975.
Analysis of the poetic characteristics of four passages the
authors consider to be among the oldest in the OT: Exodus 15,
Genesis 49, Deuteronomy 33, and 2 Samuel 22/Psalm 18.

520 D. K. Stuart. *Studies in Early Hebrew Meter*. Missoula: Scholars, 1976.
Includes history of research into Hebrew metrics. Comparison of Ugaritic and Hebrew poetry. Both are heirs to a common poetic tradition.

521 W. R. Watters. *Formula Criticism and the Poetry of the Old Testament*. BZAW, 138. Berlin: Walter de Gruyter, 1976.

Antecedents and history of formula criticism, that is, the use of word pairs in oral verse-making (work of Lord and Parry on Homer and oral poetry). Formula criticism, when adapted to biblical studies, "opens the door to a number of ways, hitherto unnoticed, of approaching classic Old Testament problems" (p. 146).

522 W. G. E. Watson. "The Pivot Pattern in Hebrew, Ugaritic and Akkadian Poetry." *ZAW* 88 (1976): 239–53.

Discussion and additional instances of M. Dahood's "double-duty modifier" (#503), which this author calls the "pivot pattern" (a word or phrase that simultaneously divides and modifies two cola). Its presence is certain but relatively infrequent.

523 D. N. Freedman. "Pottery, Poetry, and Prophecy: An Essay on Biblical Poetry." *JBL* 96 (1977): 5–26. Reprinted in Freedman's *Pottery, Poetry, and Prophecy: Studies in Early Hebrew Poetry*. Winona Lake, Ind.: Eisenbrauns, 1980, pp. 1–22 (#532).

Presentation of "two aspects of Hebrew poetry in light of recent research and discussion: (1) its character, including (a) definition; (b) sequence-dating; (c) forms and structures; (2) its function as the vehicle of revelation, including (a) pagan patterns: myth, epic, ritual, oracle; (b) Israelite adaptation: echoes and remnants of epic traditions, surviving poems; (c) continuation: worship (Psalms), wisdom (Proverbs, Job), oracles (Prophets)" (p. 6).

524 J. S. Kselman. "Semantic-Sonant Chiasmus in Biblical Poetry." *Bib* 58 (1977): 219–23.

Hebrew poetry at times combines chiasmus and assonance ("semantic-sonant chiasmus"), for example, Genesis 27:36: 't bkrty lqʾ//whnh 'th lqʾ brkty.

525 T. Collins. *Line-Forms in Hebrew Poetry: A Grammatical Approach to the Stylistic Study of the Hebrew Prophets*. Studia Pohl Series Maior, 7. Rome: Biblical Institute, 1978.

Focusing on the prophetic corpus, the author attempts "to do justice to the role of syntax [as opposed to semantic or phonetic elements] in the composition of Hebrew poetry" (p. 20).

526 M. Kessler. "Inclusio in the Hebrew Bible." *Semitics* 6 (1978): 44–49.

Inclusio must be considered with respect to its "classic" definition, that is, verbal identity with some allowances for case endings and other matters. Other types of inclusio ("approximate inclusio") include use of synonyms and structural indicators.

527 J. C. de Moor. "The Art of Versification in Ugarit and Israel II: The Formal Structure." *Ugarit-Forschungen* 10 (1978): 187–217.
     The versification of West Semitic poetry is diverse, consisting in both contraction (where larger units become smaller ones, e.g., strophes becomes verses) and expansion (e.g., a stichos consisting of two words).

528 J. P. van der Westhuizen. "Hendiadys in Biblical Hymns of Praise." *Semitics* 6 (1978): 50–57.
     Although evident, hendiadys is not a common phenomenon in hymns of praise.

529 A. Berlin. "Grammatical Aspects of Biblical Parallelism." *HUCA* 50 (1979): 17–43.
     Parallelism operates not only on the lexical-semantic level, but on the grammatical (i.e., morphological and syntactic) level as well.

530 S. A. Geller. *Parallelism in Early Biblical Poetry*. Harvard Semitic Monographs, 20. Missoula: Scholars, 1979.
     "This study aims at establishing a method for analysis of major aspects of parallelism, with emphasis on grammatical and semantic parallelism, applying this method to a number of early poetic texts and then listing and studying the results" (p. 4). Many poetic patterns have their origin in oral traditions and serve to contrast poetry ("non-casual speech") with prose ("casual speech").

531 J. T. Willis. "The Juxtaposition of Synonymous and Chiastic Parallelism in Tricola in Old Testament Hebrew Psalm Poetry." *VT* 29 (1979): 465–80.
     The author has discovered "the linking together of the first two cola of a tricola in synonymous parallelism and of the last two cola in chiastic parallelism (or vice versa), so that the middle colon is simultaneously a vital element in both" (pp. 465–66).

5.4. 1980s

532 D. N. Freedman. *Pottery, Poetry, and Prophecy: Studies in Early Hebrew Poetry*. Winona Lake, Ind.: Eisenbrauns, 1980.

Collection of nineteen of Freedman's studies in Hebrew poetry, most of which were previously published in the 1970s.

533 M. O'Connor. *Hebrew Verse Structure.* Winona Lake, Ind.: Eisenbrauns, 1980.

Technical, linguistic analysis, which abstracts the various forms of clauses in Hebrew poetry. Provides structural analysis of fourteen OT texts. Like Kugel (#534), argues against notions of meter and parallelism.

534 W. G. E. Watson. "Gender-Matched Synonymous Parallelism." *JBL* 99 (1980): 321–41.

Nouns of matching gender within a colon is a feature of biblical and ANE poetry. Gives various functions and the different classifications of this type of parallelism.

535 J. L. Kugel. *The Idea of Biblical Poetry: Parallelism and Its History.* New Haven, Conn.: Yale University Press, 1981.

Innovative study of parallelism in biblical poetry and the understanding of this phenomenon in rabbinic and medieval Jewish exegesis, and the Church Fathers. Argues that notions of poetry and meter are largely impositions of Western categories, and that the poetic line should be seen as two 'halves' (A and B), where the second half 'sharpens' or emphasizes the first, as in 'A is so, and *what's more,* B.'

536 D. Pardee. "Ugaritic and Hebrew Metrics." Pp. 113–30 in *Ugarit in Retrospect: Fifty Years of Ugarit and Ugaritic.* Edited by G. D. Young. Winona Lake, Ind.: Eisenbrauns, 1981.

Toward a definition of meter. Includes examination of systems proposed by D. Stuart (#520) and B. Margalit ("Studia Ugaritica I: Introduction to Ugaritic Prosody." *Ugarit-Forschungen* 7 [1975]: 289–313). Ugaritic poetry was likely originally recited in song form and may have been ametrical or metrical.

537 W. G. E. Watson. "Chiastic Patterns in Biblical Hebrew Poetry." Pp. 118–68 in *Chiasmus in Antiquity: Structures, Analyses, Exegesis.* Edited by J. W. Welch. Heldesheim: Gerstenberg, 1981.

Wide-ranging introduction to the phenomenon of chiasmus in OT poetry. Provides many examples. Essential function of chiasmus "is to break the monotony of persistent direct parallelism" (p. 145).

538 T. Longman III. "A Critique of Two Recent Metrical Systems." *Bib* 63 (1982): 230–54.

Lengthy examination of the syllable-counting method of determining meter (i.e., F. Cross, D. N. Freedman, D. Stuart). Brief comments on the syntactic-accentual method (e.g., the Polish linguist Jerzy Kurylowicz). The former is faulty in that it rests on textual emendation. A syntactical approach (see, too, #525) is more promising.

539 W. G. E. Watson. "Trends in the Development of Classical Hebrew Poetry: A Comparative Study." *Ugarit-Forschungen* 14 (1982): 265–77.

Comparison with extrabiblical literature to determine trends in the development of Hebrew poetry (e.g., trends toward expansion and rhyme), which will serve as a general guide for dating the texts.

540 J. Krašovec. *Antithetic Structure in Biblical Hebrew Poetry.* VTSup 35. Leiden: E. J. Brill, 1984.

Investigation of the rhetorical phenomenon of "antithesis" (not only on the level of words, but also of strophes, scenes, and speeches) in the Song of Deborah, Psalm 73 (and other psalms), prophetic and didactic literature (especially Job).

541 R. Alter. *The Art of Biblical Poetry.* New York: Basic, 1985.

The author sets out "to define the workings of the formal system of biblical poetry . . . moving from the nature of the poetic line to larger structures" (p. ix), and concludes by applying his findings to major poetic texts from representative genres of the OT. Alter's and Kugel's (#535) conclusions are similar, and this fact sparked a somewhat heated debate between them.

542 W. G. E. Watson. *Classical Hebrew Poetry: A Guide to Its Techniques.* JSOTSup 26. Sheffield: JSOT, 1984. Second Edition: 1986.

A comprehensive discussion of the poetry of the OT, including chapters on extrabiblical evidence, methodological issues involved in the study of poetry, oral poetry, meter, parallelism, stanza and strophe, verse-patterns, sound, imagery, poetic devices, and twelve indexes. The author's purpose is "to give an account of the methods and results of current scholarship, and to provide both lecturers and students with guidelines for further study" (p. 2). A concise bibliography accompanies each section. See also Watson's follow-up article in *VT* 43 (1993): 372–84.

543 A. Berlin. *The Dynamics of Biblical Parallelism.* Bloomington: Indiana University Press, 1985.

Application of R. Jakobson's linguistic work in parallelism to parallelism in biblical poetry. Discusses the nature of parallelism on four distinct but interconnected levels: grammatical, lexical, semantic, and phonological.

544　E. S. Gerstenberger. "The Lyrical Literature." Pp. 409–44 in *The Hebrew Bible and Its Modern Interpreters*. Edited by D. G. Knight and G. M. Tucker. Philadelphia: Fortress /Chico, Calif.: Scholars, 1985.

Broad discussion of poetry throughout the Hebrew Bible. Overview of a variety of general topics: Dahood and the Ugaritic evidence, the nature of biblical poetry and its genres, schools of interpretation.

545　L. Alonso Schökel. *A Manual of Hebrew Poetics*. Translated by A. Graffy. Subsidia Biblica, 11. Rome: Pontifical Biblical Institute, 1988. Original Title: *Hermeneutica de la palabra. II. Interpretación literaria de textos bíblicos*. Academia christiana, 38. Madrid: Ediciones Cristiandad, 1987.

Discusses a wide variety of topics in eleven chapters, including a historical survey, poetic genres, sounds, rhythm, parallelism, and others. Conscious synthesis of the author's previous works on the subject.

546　H. Fisch. *Poetry with a Purpose: Biblical Poetics and Interpretation*. Bloomington: Indiana University Press, 1988.

Semipopular presentation of nine biblical poetic texts. The Bible cannot simply be read as literature, since the Bible itself encourages the reader to call into question accustomed literary conventions.

547　R. D. Haak. "'Poetry' in Habakkuk 1:1–2:4?" *Journal of the American Oriental Society* 108, no. 3 (1988): 437–44.

Uses Habakkuk 1:1–2:4 as a test for J. L. Kugel's (#535) understanding of biblical poetry. Argues that "it is the interplay of the parallelism on both the semantic and grammatical levels within lines, in 'near parallelism' [across adjacent lines], and in 'distant parallelism' [across nonadjoining lines] which seems to mark this material as 'poetic'" (p. 439).

548　W. van der Meer and J. C. de Moor (eds.). *The Structural Analysis of Biblical and Canaanite Poetry*. JSOTSup 74. Sheffield: JSOT, 1988.

Fifteen essays that apply the method of poetical analysis developed by P. van der Lugt in his dissertation "Strofische structuren in de bijbels—hebreeuwse poëzie" (Kampen, 1980), which follows a ten-step approach emphasizing internal parallelism (between cola) and external parallelism (between larger structural units). See also #396.

549 D. Grossberg. *Centripetal and Centrifugal Structures in Biblical Poetry*. Society of Biblical Literature Monograph Series, 39. Atlanta: Scholars, 1989.

Analysis of the poetic composition of the Songs of Ascents, Song of Songs, and Lamentations. Biblical poetry can be categorized on a continuum from centripetal (uniform structure and tight pattern) to centrifugal (loose composition).

5.5. 1990s

550 J. W. Watts. *Psalm and Story: Inset Hymns in Hebrew Narrative*. JSOTSup 139. Sheffield: JSOT, 1992.

Discusses the function of poetic elements in narrative contexts ("inset hymns") and their role in developing plot.

551 J. C. de Moor and W. G. E. Watson (eds.). *Verse in Ancient Near Eastern Prose*. Alter Orient und Altes Testament, 42. Kevelaer: Verlag Butzon & Bercker, 1993.

Discussion of poetry vis-à-vis prose by way of twenty-two essays that cover a variety of biblical genres and extrabiblical texts.

552 J. K. Kuntz. "Recent Perspectives on Biblical Poetry." *Religious Studies Review* 19 (1993): 321–27.

Review of several recent contributions to the nature of biblical poetry. Biblical poetry is discernible from prose, but remains difficult to define.

553 R. J. Giese Jr. "Strophic Hebrew Verse as Free Verse." *JSOT* 61 (1994): 29–38.

Focuses on Exodus 15 an example of rhythmic, nonmetrical verse.

554 S. E. Gillingham. *The Poems and Psalms of the Hebrew Bible*. Oxford: Oxford University Press, 1994.

Introduction to the wide range of biblical poetry in the Psalms, Song of Songs, Job, Proverbs, and songs in narrative contexts.

555 J. K. Kuntz. "Engaging the Psalms: Gains and Trends in Recent Research." *Currents in Research: Biblical Studies* 2 (1994): 77–106.

Survey of Psalms scholarship since 1980 under a variety of headings. How the Psalms function in their canonical setting is the pressing issue.

556 W. G. E. Watson. *Traditional Techniques in Classical Hebrew Verse.* JSOTSup 170. Sheffield: Sheffield Academic, 1994.

Collection of the author's previously published works (plus three new essays) on a variety of topics, in particular parallelism, chiasmus, figurative language, and rhetorical devices. Corrections are given to his previous monograph (#542) as well as bringing his arguments up to date.

557 D. N. Freedman. "Another Look at Biblical Hebrew Poetry." Pp. 11–28 in *Directions in Biblical Hebrew Poetry.* Edited by E. R. Follis. JSOTSup 40. Sheffield: JSOT, 1997.

Hebrew poetry and prose can be distinguished on the basis of the use of certain particles. Certain kinds of Hebrew poetry are quantifiable (i.e., meter).

558 E. R. Follis (ed.). *Directions in Biblical Hebrew Poetry.* JSOTSup 40. Sheffield: JSOT, 1997.

Analysis of issues in biblical poetry (e.g., parallelism, inclusion, pseudosorites) both generally and by means of interaction with specific texts in Psalms, narrative sections, and Job.

6. Psalms

Psalms scholarship experienced a tremendous shift in emphasis around the turn of the twentieth century. Rather than being understood mainly as descriptions of the life experiences of the individual writers, they came to be understood essentially as stemming from particular settings in the life of Israel's worship. Toward that end, form-critical studies have been concerned with categorizing the individual psalms into their respective genres (e.g., royal, thanksgiving, wisdom, lament). Although some have applied these categories far too rigidly, they are nevertheless a help in aiding us to understand the respective functions these psalms might have had. More recent approaches to Psalms have investigated the question of the plan and purpose of the book as a whole. It is now a commonly held belief that the book of Psalms is not a random collection of originally isolated songs but truly a book that has its own coherent structure. Also, throughout history, Psalms has been used by the faithful as a source of one's deepest religious affections. The relevance of Psalms for today is perhaps explored more fully than for any other section of the Old Testament.

6.1. Introductions

The following items include some popular-level introductions (see, too, §6.5) as well as standard ones. Some of the works listed below treat the topic of biblical poetry, so there is some overlap here with §5.

6.1.1. General

559 S. R. Driver. *Studies in the Psalms*. London: Hodder & Stoughton, 1915.

Posthumous collection of essays on the Psalms, including method of studying the Psalms. Also includes sermons on several psalms.

560 B. D. Eerdmans. *The Hebrew Book of Psalms*. Oudtestamentische Studiën, 4. Leiden: E. J. Brill, 1947.

Primarily translations of and comments on the book of Psalms. Introduction covers general issues of scholarly interest (e.g., genre, meter, origin, titles, etc.).

561 C. L. Taylor. *Let the Psalms Speak*. Greenwich, Conn.: Seabury, 1961.

Thematic introduction to the Psalms covering the psalmist's concept of truth, the psalmist's troubles, poetry, lasting appeal of the Psalms, and their relevance for today.

562 P. Drijvers. *The Psalms: Their Structure and Meaning*. London: Burns & Oates, 1965. Original Title: *Over de Psalmen*. Utrecht: Uitgeverij Het Spectrum, 1964.

General overview of genres, origin, and poetry.

563 C. F. Barth. *Introduction to the Psalms*. Translated by R. A. Wilson. New York: Charles Scribner's Sons, 1966.

Brief discussions of twenty-two separate topics, including the genres, various themes, and introductory matters (origins, headings, authorship).

564 L. Sabourin. *The Psalms: Their Origin and Meaning*. 2 vols. Staten Island: Alba House, 1974.

Introduction to a wide variety of critical issues concerning the book as a whole (original setting, dates, theology) and the individual genres (hymn, lament, thanksgiving, royal, didactic). Includes list of psalms arranged according to genre.

565 H.-J. Kraus. *Theology of the Psalms*. Translated by K. Crim. Minneapolis: Augsburg, 1986. Original Title: *Theologie der Psalmen*. Neukirchener Verlag, 1979.

Cross-section of a number of themes in the Psalms: God, God's people, sanctuary, king, enemies, the individual. Includes discussion of Psalms in the NT.

566 C. Westermann. *The Psalms: Structure, Content and Message*. Translated by R. D. Gehrke. Minneapolis: Augsburg, 1980. Original Title: *Der Psalter*. Stuttgart: Calwer Verlag, 1967.

Discussion of the various genres: community and individual lament and praise; hymn; creation; liturgical; royal; enthronement; wisdom. Includes chapters on Psalm 119 and the NT.

567 C. H. Bullock. "Interpreting the Songs of Israel." Pp. 79–102 in *The Literature and Meaning of Scripture*. Edited by M. A. Inch and C. H. Bullock. Grand Rapids: Baker, 1981.

Approach to interpreting Psalms (and Song of Songs). Brief discussion of classifications and structure of the book. Outlines four principles of interpretation using Psalm 2 as an example.

568 J. H. Eaton. *The Psalms Come Alive: Capturing the Voice and Art of Israel's Songs*. Downers Grove: InterVarsity, 1984.

Popular introduction to issues that affect one's understanding of the Psalms: poetry, structure, music, dance, drama.

569 C. Westermann. *The Living Psalms*. Translated by J. R. Porter. Grand Rapids: Eerdmans, 1989. Original Title: *Ausgewählte Psalmen*. Göttingen: Vandenhoeck und Ruprecht, 1984.

Introductions to, translations of, and comments on various psalms considered under their respective genre headings.

570 R. Alter. "Psalms." Pp. 244–62 in *The Literary Guide to the Bible*. Edited by R. Alter and F. Kermode. Cambridge: Belknap Press of Harvard University Press, 1987.

Genre, style, structure, and themes of the Psalms.

571 T. Longman III. *How to Read the Psalms*. Downers Grove: InterVarsity, 1988.

Introduction to the genre of biblical psalms and their poetic composition. Offers interpretation of Psalms 30, 69, and 98 as examples.

572 R. Tomes. "The Psalms." Pp. 251–67 in *Creating the Old Testament: The Emergence of the Hebrew Bible*. Edited by S. Bigger. Oxford: Basil Blackwell, 1989.

Psalms in Jewish and Christian worship; history and composition; setting; nature of poetry; theology.

573 W. H. Bellinger Jr. *Psalms: Reading and Studying the Book of Praises*. Peabody, Mass.: Hendrickson, 1990.

Mainly introduces readers to the genres of the Psalms: lament, praise, royal, wisdom. Includes chapters on strategies for reading the Psalms and the relevance of the Psalms for the life of faith.

574 J. Day. *Psalms*. Old Testament Guides. Sheffield: Sheffield Academic, 1990.

Chapters on the various genres: lament, praise and thanksgiving, autumn festival, royal, and other; introductory matters, theology, and history of interpretation.

575 T. Longman III. "Psalms." Pp. 245–55 in *A Complete Literary Guide to the Bible*. Edited by L. Ryken and T. Longman III. Grand Rapids: Zondervan, 1993.

Overview of genre and poetic style.

576 J. C. McCann Jr. *A Theological Introduction to the Book of Psalms: Psalms as Torah*. Nashville: Abingdon, 1993.

The Psalter is a book of instruction (Torah) in addition to a book of prayers.

577 J. D. Pleins. *The Psalms: Songs of Tragedy, Hope, and Justice*. The Bible and Liberation: An Orbis Series on Biblical Studies. Maryknoll, N.Y.: Orbis, 1993.

Introduction to the Psalms organized under three headings: communal and individual; royal; history, wisdom, and prophecy.

578 N. M. Sarna. *Songs of the Heart: An Introduction to the Book of Psalms*. New York: Schocken, 1993.

Exposition of several Psalms (1, 8, 19, 15 and 24, 30, 48, 82, 93, 94) of different genres for the purpose of introducing the reader to the depth of religious insight the Psalter contains.

579 J. Magonet. *A Rabbi Reads the Psalms*. London: SCM, 1994.

Semipopular and insightful introduction to the world and interpretation of the Psalms and to rabbinic interpretation. Includes chapter on biblical poetry and discussions on several psalms to illustrate his points.

580 E. Zenger. "New Approaches to the Study of the Psalms." *Proceedings of the Bible Association* 17 (1994): 37–54.

Current issues in Psalms research, especially form-criticism. Composition and theology of the subgroup Psalms 25–34. The book of Psalms is meant to be read both as individual texts (patterns of conduct) and as a programmatic, coherent composition.

581 W. Brueggemann. *The Psalms of Life and Faith*. Edited by P. D. Miller Jr. Minneapolis: Fortress, 1995.

Collection of fourteen of Brueggemann's articles on a variety of topics organized under three headings: "The Psalms as

Prayer and Praise"; "Covenant and Canon as Context"; "Interpreted Psalms" (9–10, 37, 77, 109).

6.1.2. History of Scholarship

582 A. Kapelrud. "Scandinavian Research in the Psalms after Mowinckel." *Annual of the Swedish Theological Institute* 4 (1965): 74–90.

Research in Psalms carried on by some of Mowinckel's students and others (H. Birkeland, H. L. Jansen, G. Widengren, I. Engnell, H. Ringgren, G. W. Ahlström, S. Holm-Nielsen).

583 D. J. A. Clines. "Psalm Research since 1955: I. The Psalms and the Cult." *TynBul* 18 (1967): 103–26.

Survey of literature from 1955 to 1966: cultic origin of the Psalms; enthronement festival; role of the king.

584 D. J. A. Clines. "Psalm Research since 1955: II. The Literary Genres." *TynBul* 20 (1969): 105–25.

Sequel to *TynBul* 18 (1967): 103–26 (#583). Covers literature on genre from 1955 to 1968.

585 E. S. Gerstenberger. "Psalms." Pp. 179–223 in *Old Testament Form Criticism*. Edited by J. H. Hayes. San Antonio: Trinity University Press, 1974.

Concise summary of the history of form-critical research and the major psalm genres.

586 B. S. Childs. "Reflections on the Modern Study of the Psalms." Pp. 377–88 in *Magnalia Dei: The Mighty Acts of God: Essays on the Bible and Archaeology in Memory of G. Ernest Wright*. Edited by F. M. Cross et al. Garden City, N.Y.: Doubleday, 1976.

A shift is needed in Psalms study from questions that have dominated past scholarship, namely, greater emphasis on canonical form.

587 R. E. Clements. "Interpreting the Psalms." Pp. 76–98 in Clements' *One Hundred Years of Old Testament Interpretation*. Philadelphia: Westminster, 1976.

History of scholarship covering the primary issues.

588 P. D. Miller Jr. *Interpreting the Psalms*. Philadelphia: Fortress, 1986.

Current issues in interpretation, historical content, poetry, laments, hymns. Exposition of Psalms 1, 2, 14, 22, 23, 82, 90,

127, 130, 139. See also Miller's "Current Issues in Psalms Studies." *Word and World* 5, no. 2 (1985): 132–43.

589 K. Seybold. *Introducing the Psalms.* Translated by R. G. Dunphy. Edinburgh: T. & T. Clark, 1990. Original Title: *Die Psalmen, Eine Einführung.* Stuttgart: W. Kohlhammer Verlag, 1986.

General introduction covering a wide range of topics, including historical backgrounds, literary form, genre classification, and ANE parallels.

590 J. K. Kuntz. "Engaging the Psalms: Gains and Trends in Recent Research." *Currents in Research: Biblical Studies* 2 (1994): 77–106.

Overview of several topics of current scholarly research into the Psalms: introductions to the Psalms, biblical poetry, commentaries, form-critical approaches, canonical shaping of the Psalter, theology, studies of specific psalms.

591 T. Wittstruck. *The Book of Psalms: An Annotated Bibliography.* Books of the Bible, 5. Garland Reference Library of the Humanities, 1413. New York: Garland, 1994.

Contains 4,971 books and articles; comprehensive from 1940–93, selective before 1940. Includes author index.

591 J. L. Mays. "Past, Present, and Prospect in Psalm Study." Pp. 147–56 in *Old Testament Interpretation: Past Present and Future.* Edited by J. L. Mays, D. L. Peterson, and K. H. Richards. Nashville: Abingdon, 1995.

Overview of Psalms research in the twentieth century, which has focused on the question of genre, and changes in directions of research more recently, that is, the importance of contexts other than Sitz-im-Leben.

6.2. Original Setting and Purpose

The question of who wrote the Psalms and for what purpose was largely moot until the turn of the twentieth century. A particular psalm was thought to have been written by the person to whom it is attributed in the superscription. The content of the psalm then tells us something about that writer's life and experience as he struggles in his trials or rejoices in God's presence. These psalms apply to modern readers insofar as their experiences approximate those of the psalmist. If a superscription is missing, the interpreter's job is to discern as closely as possible the likely historical circumstance that gave rise to the psalm in question. But beginning in the nineteenth century, the Psalms came to be understood as reflections of communal Israelite worship, many of which were post-Davidic compositions (for some scholars, stemming even from the Maccabean era). Building on the work of others, H. Gunkel developed a fresh, and, as it turns out, influential approach to Psalms interpretation, which classified the Psalms into different types (*Gattung*). Although some of the Psalms may have ultimately been composed as expressions of personal piety, the Psalms as a whole should be understood in the context of their use in the corporate worship of Israel (although the destruction of the temple gave occasion for these Psalms to move beyond the cultic boundary and came to express personal piety). Much of subsequent scholarship has sought to determine more precisely the settings for either the genres as a whole or for individual psalms.

593 H. Gunkel. *The Psalms: A Form-Critical Introduction.* Translated by T. M. Horner. Philadelphia: Fortress, 1967. Original Title: *Die Religion in Geschichte und Gegenwart.* Tübingen: J. C. B. Mohr (Paul Siebeck), 1930.

Introduction to Gunkel's ground-breaking approach to Psalms research: delimit the literary unit, identify its genre *(Gattung)*, trace its preliterary origin, determine its setting in personal or communal life.

594 M. Buttenweiser. *The Psalms: Chronologically Treated with a New Translation.* The Library of Biblical Studies, 1938. Reprint: New York: KTAV, 1969.

Divides the Psalter into preexilic, exilic, and postexilic categories. By treating the Psalms in this way, the author shows how they "mirror . . . the spiritual growth of Israel" (p. xxxix). Contains prolegomenon by N. Sarna, which overviews history of Psalms scholarship.

595 J. H. Patton. *Canaanite Parallels in the Book of Psalms.* Baltimore: Johns Hopkins, 1944.

Comparison of Ugaritic and Hebrew parallels in the Psalms with respect to literary form (prosody, language, grammar), "thought patterns" (e.g., El; Rider on the Clouds), and vocabulary.

596 J. Paterson. *The Praises of Israel: Studies Literary and Religious in the Psalms.* New York: Charles Scribner's Sons, 1950.

Interpretation of ten psalms that are representative of respective genres. The Psalms "originate in the religious cult and are associated with the worship of the community" (p. 29).

597 S. Mowinckel. *The Psalms in Israel's Worship*. Translated by
D. R. AP-Thomas. 2 vols. Nashville: Abingdon, 1962. Original
Title: *Offersang og Sangoffer*. Oslo: H. Aschehoug, 1951.
Influential form-critical study of the cultic setting of Israel's
psalms. Emphasis on cultic and sociological issues. Employed
"New Year's Festival" hypothesis to explain many psalms.
Individualistic psalms stem from private worship. "Learned
psalmographers" were responsible for instructional psalms
rather than cultic psalms.

598 C. Westermann. *The Praise of God in the Psalms*. Translated by
K. R. Crim. Richmond: John Knox, 1965. Original Title: *Das
Loben Gottes in den Psalmen*. Göttingen: Vandenhoeck und
Ruprecht, 1961.
Influential form-critical study of the various psalm categories.
Comparison to Babylonian psalms. Each biblical psalm in each
category generally displays the same basic structure.

599 R. C. Culley. *Oral Formulaic Language in the Biblical Psalms*.
Toronto: University of Toronto Press, 1967.
Follows A. B. Lord and M. Parry's work on oral formulaic language in Homeric literature. Argues for presence of this same
phenomenon in the Psalms, and hence for their origins as oral
compositions rather than written works.

600 E. B. Smick. "Ugaritic and the Theology of the Psalms." Pp.
104–16 in *New Perspectives on the Old Testament*. Edited by
J. B. Payne. Waco: Word, 1970.
Evaluation of the Northwest Semitic data for the Psalms and
their relevance for the theology of the Psalms, particularly
immortality and resurrection and messianism and divine sov-
ereignty.

601 B. S. Childs. "Psalm Titles and Midrashic Exegesis." *JSS* 16 (1971):
137–50.
Psalm titles are not only important in discussions concerning the historical settings of the psalms, but "represent an
early reflection of how the Psalms as a collection of sacred literature were understood. . . . In this sense the titles form an
important link in the history of exegesis" (p. 137).

602 D. Anders-Richards. *The Drama of the Psalms*. Valley Forge, Pa.:
Judson, 1972.
Many psalms should be understood "as parts of the text of cul-
tic dramas or national liturgies used in the assemblies and fes-

tivals of Israel" (p. 48). Summarizes evidence for an OT New Year's Festival.

603 H. Ringgren. *The Faith of the Psalmists.* Philadelphia: Fortress, 1974.

Psalms represent "piety nourished in the cult" (p. xxii) and "are our best source for understanding the religious life of ancient Israel" (p. xviii).

604 J. H. Eaton. "The Psalms and Israelite Worship." Pp. 238–73 in *Tradition and Interpretation: Essays by Members of the Society for Old Testament Study.* Edited by G. W. Anderson. Oxford: Clarendon, 1979.

"The core of the Psalter was composed for national and royal worship at the Temple" (p. 263), specifically the fall festal season and national crises.

605 A. R. Johnson. *The Cultic Prophet and Israel's Psalmody.* Cardiff: University of Wales Press, 1979.

During the monarchy and for two centuries later there existed in Israel an official cult prophet who served both as a spokesman for Yahweh and as a representative of the people to Yahweh. During the exile, these prophets lost prestige and were subsumed under levitical categories. (See also the author's earlier, briefer work by the same title, Cardiff, 1944.)

606 P. D. Miller Jr. "Psalms and Inscriptions." Pp. 311–32 in *Congress Volume: Vienna, 1980.* Edited by J. Emerton. VTSup 32. Leiden: E. J. Brill, 1981.

Compares Psalms and contemporary inscriptions "to let them reflect off one another as a way of seeking to understand both Psalms and inscriptions more clearly and to demonstrate the continuity of these non-biblical archaic texts with the biblical tradition as it is carried down to the present" (p. 312).

607 C. Westermann. *Praise and Lament in the Psalms.* Translated by K. R. Crim and R. N. Soulen. Atlanta: John Knox, 1981. Original Title: *Lob und Klage in den Psalmen.* Göttingen: Vandenhoeck und Ruprecht, 1977.

Fifth edition of *Das Loben Gottes in den Psalmen* (#597) augmented by three additional essays (see p. 3 for bibliography), two on lament and one on the formation of the Psalter.

608 M. D. Goulder. *The Psalms of the Sons of Korah.* JSOTSup 20. Sheffield: JSOT, 1982.

Evidence from the Psalms of Korah (42–49; 84–85; 87–88) suggest an original setting in a week-long autumnal festival in
Dan in the ninth and eighth centuries in which these psalms
were used in a specific sequence.

609 A. M. Cooper. "The Life and Times of King David according to
the Book of Psalms." Pp. 117–31 in *The Poet and the Historian:
Essays in Literary and Historical Biblical Criticism.* Edited by
R. E. Friedman. HSS, 26. Chico, Calif.: Scholars, 1983.
Psalms give little aid in understanding the historical
David. We are left to read the Psalter either canonically or
ahistorically.

610 E. Haglund. *Historical Motifs in the Psalms.* Coniectanae biblica, Old Testament Series, 23. Lund: Gleerup, 1984.
Discussion of the cultic function of the historical psalms.
These psalms are used as motivations for praise, meditation,
and trust in God.

611 J. L. Mays. "The David of the Psalms." *Int* 40 (1986): 143–55.
The David of the Psalms is an "intra-textual reality" rather
than a historical one. "The Davidic connection directs the
reader to think of each psalm and the entire Psalter as an
expression of faith in the reign of the Lord as the sphere in
which individual and corporate life is lived" (p. 155).

612 H. P. Nasuti. *Tradition History and the Psalms of Asaph.* SBLDS,
88. Atlanta: Scholars, 1988.
Linguistic and form-critical analysis. These psalms stem from
"the Ephraimite tradition stream" (p. 193). The Asaphites were
"distinctive and durable participants in both the Jerusalem
cult and the larger social and theological history of ancient
Israel" (p. 195).

613 M. D. Goulder. *The Prayers of David (Psalms 51–72): Studies in
the Psalter,* II. JSOTSup 102, Sheffield: JSOT, 1990.
These psalms were prayers "written 'for David', in his life-
time, by one of his closest attendants, a priest; . . . they cover
the last years of his life serially from the death of Uriah to the
succession of Solomon; . . . the Selahs in the text provided
opportunities for the recitation of sections of the earliest form
of the 'Succession Narrative'" (p. 9).

614 G. A. Rendsburg. *Linguistic Evidence for the Northern Origin of
Selected Psalms.* Society of Biblical Literature Monograph Series,
43. Atlanta: Scholars, 1990.

Psalms 9–10, 16, 29, 36, 45, 53, 58, 74, 116, 132, 133, 140, and 141, as well as the Psalms of Korah and Asaph, likely originated in northern Israel.

615 S. Gelander. "Convention and Originality: Identification of the Situation in the Psalms." *VT* 42 (1992): 302–16.

The setting of the Psalms is not universally cultic. Some psalms exhibit evidence of a personal setting.

616 W. L. Holladay. *The Psalms through Three Thousand Years: Prayerbook of a Cloud of Witnesses*. Minneapolis: Augsburg/Fortress, 1993.

Overview of the use of the Psalms over three millennia. Nineteen chapters organized under three headings: reconstruction of original settings; the Psalter through history; current issues.

617 J. L. Mays. "The Question of Context in Psalm Interpretation." Pp. 14–20 in *The Shape and Shaping of the Psalter*. Edited by J. C. McCann. JSOTSup 159. Sheffield: JSOT, 1993.

Proposes "five kinds of data that can be used to construct a description of the understanding, mentality and piety that led to and used the book of Psalms" (p. 16). See also R. E. Murphy's follow-up article in the same volume ("Reflections on Contextual Interpretation of the Psalms," pp. 21–28).

618 L. D. Crow. *The Psalms of Ascents (Psalms 120–134): Their Place in Israelite History and Religion*. SBLDS, 148. Atlanta: Scholars, 1996.

History of interpretation, exegesis, redaction, and sociohistorical setting of the psalms of ascent. Final redaction during Persian period; became "a sort of devotional handbook for pilgrims" (p. 157).

619 M. R. Hauge. *Between Sheol and Temple: Motif Structure and Function in the I-Psalms*. JSOTSup 178. Sheffield: Sheffield Academic, 1996.

The "I" in the Psalms is to be understood in the context of "religious language, expressing an interpretative symbol-system of conceptual character" (p. 281) rather than biographical categories.

6.3. Structure

The poetic style of the Psalms has certainly received a great deal of attention. Although a few works are cited here, §5 should be consulted for fuller bibliographic information on this important subject. The macrostructure of the Psalter is a topic that has attracted a fair amount of attention in recent decades, and may be thought of as moving beyond the limited scope of form-critical approaches. Ultimately, it is not enough to offer explanations for cultic settings of certain psalms, nor simply to offer plausible dates of composition. Sooner or later the question arises, "What *is* the book of Psalms and why does it look the way it does?" Not surprisingly, theories abound to explain the final form of the book, but certain elements are routinely agreed upon, namely, the Psalter is divided into five "books" and there is sufficient evidence in the Psalter to demonstrate a purposeful plan for the book as a whole.

6.3.1. Poetic Style

620   R. G. Boling. "'Synonymous' Parallelism in the Psalms." *JSS* 5 (1960): 221–55.

Analysis of "the standard metrical patterns of the Psalter, with special attention to the combinations and sequences in which words are used in parallelism" (pp. 221–22).

621   J. J. Goldingay. "Repetition and Variation in the Psalms." *JQR* 68 (1977–78): 146–51.

Variation in psalmic refrains is not evidence of textual corruption but of the writers' style and should not be glossed over by commentators or translators.

622   P. R. Raabe. *Psalm Structure: A Study of Psalms with Refrains.* JSOTSup 104. Sheffield: JSOT, 1990.

Discussion of Psalms 42–43, 46, 49, 56, 57, and 59, all of which have refrains, to understand the "building blocks" of psalms in general.

623   P. R. Raabe. "Deliberate Ambiguity in the Psalter." *JBL* 110 (1991): 213–27.

Psalms contain deliberate ambiguity on the lexical, phonetic, and grammatical levels. Eliminates the need for some textual emendation.

624   G. A. Mikre-Sellassie. "Metonymy in the Book of Psalms." *The Bible Translator* 44 (1993): 418–25.

Catalog of the uses of metonymy in the Psalter.

6.3.2. Macrostructure

625 J. P. Brennan. "Some Hidden Harmonies of the Fifth Book of Psalms." Pp. 126–58 in *Essays in Honor of Joseph P. Brennan.* Edited by R. F. McNamara. Rochester: St. Bernard's Seminary, 1976.

Psalms must be understood in relation to each other. They have been carefully arranged so that originally independent compositions "now comment upon and or respond to one another" (p. 127). Comments briefly on Psalms 107–150, highlighting development and links between them.

626 G. H. Wilson. "Evidence of Editorial Divisions in the Hebrew Psalter." *VT* 34 (1984): 337–52.

The shape of the Psalter is the result of conscious, pervading editorial work, as can be seen by (1) the use of author designations; (2) function of genre categories in the headings; (3) the use of *hllwyh* and *hwdw* Psalms.

627 G. H. Wilson. *The Editing of the Hebrew Psalter.* SBLDS, 76. Chico: Scholars, 1985.

Examination of the Psalms and the Qumran psalm manuscripts for evidence of editorial shaping in the OT book of Psalms. Demonstrates among other things that the division of Psalms into "books" is the result of purposeful editorial activity. Final form is exilic/postexilic and addresses the failure of the monarchy.

628 G. H. Wilson. "The Function of 'Untitled' Psalms in the Hebrew Psalter." *ZAW* 97 (1985): 404–13.

Six untitled psalms in Books I–III (Psalms 1, 2, 10, 33, 43, 71) are discussed. One reason they remain untitled by the Psalms editor is an effort to maintain a tie with the immediately preceding psalm. See #625.

629 G. H. Wilson. "The Use of the Royal Psalms at the 'Seams' of the Hebrew Psalter." *JSOT* 35 (1986): 85–94.

Books IV and V of the Psalter are additions that reflect on the dismay over the failure of the Davidic covenant and express faith in God's direct protection without royal mediation.

630 T. Collins. "Decoding the Psalms: A Structural Approach to the Psalter." *JSOT* 37 (1987): 41–60.

"Our brief outline of the different types of hidden structure discoverable in Psalms indicates clearly that the book has an inner cohesion [its purpose is didactic], despite the random surface arrangement of elements" (p. 56).

631 S. J. L. Croft. *The Identity of the Individual in the Psalms.* JSOTSup 44. Sheffield: JSOT, 1987.

The individual psalms were most often written for use in the temple cult. Often the king used these psalms for leading public worship. Other individual psalms were intended for the ordinary worshiper. Other individuals include cult ministers, prophets, wisdom teachers, and temple singers.

632 J. M. O'Brien. "Because God Heard My Voice: The Individual Thanksgiving Psalm and Vow-Fulfillment." Pp. 281–98 in *The Listening Heart: Essays in Wisdom and the Psalms in Honor of Roland E. Murphy, O. Carm.* Edited by K. G. Hoglund et al. JSOTSup 58. Sheffield: JSOT, 1987.

Emphasis on public fulfillment of the individual's vow in the temple context. Compares Phoenician/Punic votive stelae and biblical lament psalms, in particular, Psalms 66 and 116.

633 D. M. Howard Jr. "Editorial Activity in the Psalter: A State-of-the-Field Survey." *Word and World* 9 (1989): 274–85. Reprinted in J. C. McCann's *The Shape and Shaping of the Psalter.* JSOTSup 159. Sheffield: JSOT, 1993, pp. 52–70.

Most studies that treat the editorial shaping of the Psalms "approach it at either the higher level of collections and large, organizing principles, or at the lower level of links between adjacent psalms, and some do on both levels" (p. 284).

634 M. S. Smith. "The Levitical Compilation of the Psalter." *ZAW* 103 (1991): 258–63.

Internal and external evidence points toward levitical responsibility for the shape of the Psalter.

635 J. H. Walton. "Psalms: A Cantata about the Davidic Covenant." *Journal of the Evangelical Theological Society* 34 (1991): 21–31.

The Psalter is organized by content as a cantata around the theme of the Davidic covenant.

636 S. L. Cook. "Apocalypticism and the Psalter." *ZAW* 104 (1992): 82–99.

Apocalyptic elements can be found in composition and redaction of the Psalms. Suggests postexilic setting for this apocalyptic redaction.

637 M. S. Smith. "The Theology of the Redaction of the Psalter: Some Observations." *ZAW* 104 (1992): 408–12.

Whereas Books I–III of the Psalter center around David's reign, Books IV–V focus on a kingly reign that has as its basis Yahweh's ultimate rule over Israel.

638 G. H. Wilson. "The Shape of the Book of Psalms." *Int* 46 (1992): 129–42.

Investigation of the placement of specific psalms (e.g., royal, wisdom) in the broader outline of the "five books" of the Psalter. Helps discern the shape of the Psalter as a whole, which is a movement from lament to praise.

639 J. C. McCann (ed.). *The Shape and Shaping of the Psalter.* JSOTSup 159. Sheffield: JSOT, 1993.

Nine essays focusing on the literary unity of the Psalter.

640 J. C. McCann "Books I–III and the Editorial Purpose of the Hebrew Psalter." Pp. 93–107 in *The Shape and Shaping of the Psalter*. Edited by J. C. McCann. JSOTSup 159. Sheffield: JSOT, 1993.

Follows on G. H. Wilson's *The Editing of the Hebrew Psalter* (#627) for further evidence in Books I–III of the Psalter that the purpose of the final form "was to address the apparent failure of the Davidic covenant in light of the exile, the diaspora, . . . and the postexilic era" (p. 93).

641 P. D. Miller Jr. "The Beginning of the Psalter." Pp. 83–92 in *The Shape and Shaping of the Psalter*. Edited by J. C. McCann. JSOTSup 159. Sheffield: JSOT, 1993.

Psalms 1 and 2 introduce the Psalter, especially Book I.

642 G. H. Wilson. "Shaping the Psalter: A Consideration of Editorial Linkage in the Book of Psalms." Pp. 72–82 in *The Shape and Shaping of the Psalter*. Edited by J. C. McCann. JSOTSup 159. Sheffield: JSOT, 1993.

Each of the five books of the Psalter has a frame (particularly royal covenant and wisdom), as does the Psalter as a whole.

643 G. H. Wilson. "Understanding the Purposeful Arrangements of Psalms in the Psalter: Pitfalls and Promise." Pp. 42–51 in *The Shape and Shaping of the Psalter*. Edited by J. C. McCann. JSOTSup 159. Sheffield: JSOT, 1993.

Survey and critique of recent literature on the literary unity of the Psalter. Accurate genre grouping and investigation of

> linguistic/thematic connections can lead to some answers
> concerning the nature of the shaping of the Psalter.

644 R. T. Beckwith. "The Early History of the Psalter." *TynBul* 46
(1995): 1–27.
> The Psalter was originally divided into three sections (books),
> not five. The first consisted of Psalms of David; the second,
> mostly Elohistic Psalms of David and the Levites; and the
> third, Psalms of David and from other periods.

645 J. F. D. Creach. *The Choice of Yahweh as Refuge and the Editing of the Hebrew Psalter.* JSOTSup 217. Sheffield: Sheffield Academic, 1996.
> "The ideas expressed by ḥāsâ/maḥseh and a related field of
> words ('refuge') represents an editorial interest that may be
> observed throughout the Psalter" (p. 17).

646 N. Whybray. *Reading the Psalms as a Book.* JSOTSup 222.
Sheffield: Sheffield Academic, 1996.
> The book of Psalms should be read as a book merely than as
> a "collection." Surveys history of research regarding compo-
> sition theories. Neither wisdom, kingship, nor ritual sacrifice
> serves as an organizing principle. The ultimate purpose for the
> present arrangement goes beyond the available evidence.

6.4. Genres

Of the various genres identified in the Psalms, three have been frequently discussed in the scholarly literature: wisdom, royal, and
lament Psalms.

6.4.1. Wisdom

647 S. Mowinckel. "Psalms and Wisdom." Pp. 205–24 in *Wisdom in
Israel and in the Ancient Near East: Presented to Professor
Harold Henry Rowley.* Edited by M. Noth and D. W. Thomas.
VTSup 3. Leiden: E. J. Brill, 1955.
> Wisdom (i.e., noncultic) psalms "originated in the circles of
> the 'wise men,' the learned leaders of the 'wisdom schools'"
> (p. 206), which the author refers to as "learned psalmography."

648 J. K. Kuntz. "The Canonical Wisdom Psalms of Ancient Israel:
Their Rhetorical, Thematic, and Formal Dimensions." Pp.
186–222 in *Rhetorical Criticism: Essays in Honor of James*

Muilenburg. Edited by J. J. Jackson and M. Kessler. Pittsburgh Theological Monograph Series, 1. Pittsburgh: Pickwick, 1974.

Outlines the elemental characteristics of wisdom psalms. Includes brief history of scholarship. The Sitz im Leben of psalmic wisdom must be approached with "considerable openness" (p. 222).

649 R. E. Murphy. "A Consideration of the Classification 'Wisdom Psalms.'" VTSup 9 (1962): 156–67. Reprinted in J. L. Crenshaw's *Studies in Ancient Israelite Wisdom.* New York: KTAV, 1976, pp. 456–67.

Argues on the basis of content, form, and motifs for including Psalms 1, 32, 34, 37, 49, 112, and 128 in the category of wisdom psalms.

650 A. R. Ceresko. "The Sage in the Psalms." Pp. 217–30 in *The Sage in Israel and the Ancient Near East.* Edited by J. G. Gammie and L. G. Perdue. Winona Lake, Ind.: Eisenbrauns, 1990.

Evidence from the Psalms suggests various aspects of the sage's profile: "the veneration of torah, the interest in prayer, the concern with order, the focus on writing, reading, and the written word as a medium of God's revelation, and the sage's self-consciousness as an author" (p. 230). Discusses wisdom influence on the shaping of the book of Psalms.

651 S. Terrien. "Wisdom in the Psalter." Pp. 51–72 in *In Search of Wisdom: Essays in Memory of John G. Gammie.* Edited by L. G. Perdue et al. Louisville: Westminster/John Knox, 1993.

Discussion of wisdom themes, especially "torah" psalms. Final editors of the Psalter may have "put a wisdom stamp upon the Psalter as scripture" (p. 72).

6.4.2. Royal

652 K. R. Crim. *The Royal Psalms.* Richmond: John Knox, 1962.

Discussion of kingship in Israel and an exposition of the royal psalms (2, 18, 20, 21, 45, 72, 89, 101, 110, 144). Royal psalms "played a leading role in keeping the expectation of the Messiah in the thoughts of people [during the Second Temple period]" (p. 127).

653 J. D. W. Watts. "Yahweh Malak Psalms." *Theologische Zeitschrift* 21 (1965): 341–48.

Discusses which psalms should be properly classified as "Yahweh Malak" psalms.

654 A. R. Johnson. *Sacral Kingship in Ancient Israel.* Second Edition. Cardiff: University of Wales Press, 1967.
Discussion of the psalms that celebrate the kingship of Yahweh and royal psalms. Israelite kings, in particular, David, were "regarded as potent extension[s] of the divine personality" (p. 14).

655 J. H. Eaton. *Kingship and the Psalms.* Second Edition. Sheffield: JSOT, 1986. Original Publisher: Studies in Biblical Theology. Second Series, 32. Naperville, Ill.: Alec R. Allenson, 1976.
Argues for extensive royal interpretation of the Psalms (contra H. Gunkel, *Die Königspsalmen und Einleitung in die Psalmen*). Divides royal psalms into those that have a clear royal content and those not so clear. Brings all this information to bear on the question of the setting and royal idea of these psalms.

656 J. F. Healey. "The Immortality of the King: Ugarit and the Psalms." *Orientalia* 53 (1984): 245–54.
"The evidence of immortality in some psalms is frequently and most plausibly to be interpreted as a reflection of royal ideology, as ideology derived in a partly demythologized form from Canaanite tradition" (p. 253).

657 J. I. Durham. "The King as 'Messiah' in the Psalms." *Review and Expositor* 81 (1984): 425–35.
Messianic (i.e., royal) psalms, in their original context, refer to the Israelite king. The king is the divine representative of Yahweh. These psalms are applicable to Christ, although they do not speak of him directly.

658 J. L. Mays. *The Lord Reigns: A Theological Handbook to the Psalms.* Louisville: Westminster/John Knox, 1994.
Central message of the Psalter is the sovereign reign of Yahweh. The Psalms are liturgical texts that serve as instructional guides for praise and worship. See Mays' previous essay "The Centre of the Psalms," *Language, Theology, and the Bible: Essays in Honour of James Barr* (ed. S. E. Balentine and J. Barton; Oxford: Clarendon, 1994), pp. 231–46. See also *Int* 47 (1993): 117–26.

6.4.3. Laments

659 C. Westermann. "The Role of the Lament in the Theology of the Old Testament." Translated by R. N. Soulen. *Int* 28 (1974): 20–38.

Man's cry of distress results in praise when God delivers him. The role of lament has been largely lost in the Christian tradition of the West.

660 P. D. Miller Jr. "Trouble and Woe: Interpreting the Biblical Laments." *Int* 37 (1983): 32–45.

"The interpretive task is not tied to the search for a single explanation for a particular lament, but can center in opening up through different stories and moments examples of the human plight that may be articulated through the richly figurative but stereotypical language of the laments" (p. 45).

661 W. H. Bellinger Jr. *Psalmody and Prophecy.* JSOTSup 27. Sheffield: JSOT, 1984.

Study of lament Psalms (individual and communal) as well as lament in Habakkuk and Joel. "There are clearly significant relationships between psalmody and prophecy in terms of form, vocabulary and function" (p. 94).

662 A. Aejmelaeus. *The Traditional Prayer in the Psalms.* BZAW, 167. Berlin/New York: de Gruyter, 1986.

Analysis of the central element of individual complaint psalm, which is the prayer (speech to God). "Appeal to God in a prayer and confidence in him seem to form the framework in which complaint was regarded as acceptable" (p. 11).

663 T. W. Cartledge. "Conditional Vows in the Psalms of Lament: A New Approach to an Old Problem." Pp. 77–94 in *The Listening Heart: Essays in Wisdom and the Psalms in Honor of Roland E. Murphy, O. Carm.* Edited by K. G. Hoglund et al. JSOTSup 58. Sheffield: JSOT, 1987.

Review of previous attempts to account for the "abrupt shift from deep lament to joyous praise" in Psalms 6, 13, 22, 28, 31, 54, 56, 59, 61, 71, 94, 109 (p. 77). The praise element may best be understood as a conditional vow, "which functions to motivate God to action" (p. 86).

664 C. C. Broyles. *The Conflict of Faith and Experience in the Psalms: A Form-Critical and Theological Study.* JSOTSup 52. Sheffield: JSOT, 1989.

Analysis of lament psalms, which are of two categories: plea (praise God) and complaint (charge God with unfaithfulness). The latter emerge from some individual or communal distress.

665 P. W. Ferris. *The Genre of Communal Lament in the Bible and the Ancient Near East.* SBLDS, 127. Atlanta: Scholars, 1992.
Compares biblical and Mesopotamian communal lament genre, and concludes that they are independent of each other. Includes discussions on Psalms 31, 35, 42–43, 44, 56, 60, 69, 74, 77, 79, 80, 83, 85, 94, 102, 109, 137, and 142 and Lamentations.

666 E. Zenger. *A God of Vengeance? Understanding the Psalms of Divine Wrath.* Translated by Linda M. Maloney. Louisville: Westminster/John Knox, 1996. Original Title: *Ein Gott der Rache: Feindpsalmen Verstehen.* Verlag Herder, Freiburg, 1994.
Vengeance Psalms (12, 139, 58, 83, 137, 44, 109) are actually laments to be employed by the oppressed. Hence, they are not incompatible with the NT message and are of practical use for the church today.

6.5. Use of the Psalms Today

Along with Proverbs, the Psalms are part of the OT that seem to lend themselves most easily to modern-day use. The following works are not, however, limited to popular expositions of Psalms. Some represent more sophisticated hermeneutical reflections on the proper use of the Psalms in a variety of contexts. As long as there have been psalms, people have been asking how they can appropriate their message. This is no less true today than it was in biblical times.

667 D. A. Redding. *Songs in the Night: Psalms of David.* Westwood, N.J.: Fleming H. Revell, 1970.
Devotional studies on all 150 psalms.

668 B. W. Anderson. *Out of the Depths: The Psalms Speak for Us Today.* Philadelphia: Westminster, 1974.
Application of form-criticism to individual and group devotional study of the Psalms. Organized according to genre. Includes glossary and index of the genres of each of the psalms.

669 W. Brueggemann. "Psalms and the Life of Faith: A Suggested Typology of Function." *JSOT* 17 (1980): 3–32.
The author asks, "What has been the function and intention of the Psalms as they were shaped, transmitted and repeatedly used?" (p. 3). Applies P. Ricoeur's understanding of the dynamics of life as "a movement, dialectic but not regular or patterned, of disorientation and reorientation" (p. 5). (See also J.

Goldingay. "The Dynamic Cycle of Praise and Prayer in the Psalms." *JSOT* 20 [1981]: 85–90.)

670 R. E. Murphy. "The Faith of the Psalmist." *Int* 34 (1980): 229–39.
The book of Psalms is a "school of prayer" that shows us how to approach God with "honest realism" (p. 229).

671 W. Brueggemann. *Praying the Psalms*. Winona, Minn.: Saint Mary's, 1982.
Focuses on the function of language in the use of the Psalms and the Christian use of what is obviously Jewish spiritual literature.

672 W. Brueggemann. *The Message of the Psalms: A Theological Commentary*. Augsburg Old Testament Studies. Minneapolis: Augsburg, 1984.
"Postcritical" interpretation of selected psalms that emphasizes the needed interaction between devotional and scholarly reading. Psalms can be divided into three general themes: poems of orientation, disorientation, and new orientation.

673 J. Limburg. *Psalms for Sojourners: Strength and Hope for Today from the Treasury of Old Testament Prayer*. Minneapolis: Augsburg, 1986.
Devotional introduction to the various genres: laments, psalms of trust, pilgrimage, hymns, creation.

674 G. Appleton. *Understanding the Psalms*. London: Mowbray, 1987.
Brief meditations on all 150 psalms.

675 M. S. Smith. *Psalms: The Divine Journey*. New York: Paulist, 1987.
The book's purpose is to "establish a dialogue between our experience and [the Israelites'] experience of God" by recovering "the psalmists' language [i.e., poetry], world view and religious experience [i.e., Jerusalem and the Temple]" (p. 5). See also *Int* 46 (1992): 156–66.

676 W. Brueggemann. *Israel's Praise: Doxology against Idolatry and Ideology*. Philadelphia: Fortress, 1988.
Pursues the question of "how the sociology of the Psalms, the work of the pastoral office, and the competing symbolizations converge in our present circumstance" (p. x).

677 W. Brueggemann. *Abiding Astonishment: Psalms, Modernity, and the Making of History*. Literary Currents in Biblical Interpretation. Louisville: Westminster/John Knox, 1991.

Historical psalms are not merely records of what happened, but recitals of what happened, serving to mediate Israel's remembered past to their own situation. They function the same way today.

678 J. L. Mays. " A Question of Identity: The Threefold Hermeneutic of Psalmody." *ASTJ* 46 (1991): 87–94.

Psalms are best appropriated by the church if they are read as witnesses to Christ's humanity and in community, both vicariously and to create a community consciousness.

679 J. C. McCann Jr. "The Psalms as Instruction." *Int* 46 (1992): 117–28.

When seen as a unified literary product rather than simply a collection of cultic compositions, the book of Psalms teaches its readers that the Lord reigns and is worthy of praise.

680 R. E. Murphy. "The Psalms and Worship." *Ex Auditu* 8 (1992): 23–31.

Explores how Christians can appropriate the Psalms for worship. Original setting is important but not wholly determinative. Canonical setting of the Psalter affects the interpretation of any individual psalm. The NT should not wholly determine the meaning of a psalm.

681 M. V. Rienstra. *Swallow's Nest: A Feminine Reading of the Psalms*. Grand Rapids: Eerdmans; New York: Friendship; Leominster, England: Gracewig, 1992.

Feminist translations of the Psalms for devotional purposes for women.

682 G. T. Sheppard. "Theology and the Book of Psalms." *Int* 46 (1992): 143–55.

David's prayers are essentially petitions of refuge. They depict his honest struggles and as such present him as an approachable human figure.

683 W. C. Kaiser. *The Journey Isn't Over: The Pilgrim Psalms for Life's Challenges and Joys*. Grand Rapids: Baker, 1993.

Popular exposition and present application of the psalms of ascent.

684 R. E. Murphy. *The Psalms Are Yours*. New York: Paulist, 1993.

Introduction to the Psalter: interpretive approaches, theology, praying the Psalms. Includes brief commentary on each psalm.

685 D. B. Allender and T. Longman III. *The Cry of the Soul: How Our Emotions Reveal Our Deepest Questions about God.* Colorado Springs, Colo.: NavPress, 1994.

Psalms help us understand that all our emotions reveal to us both how we understand God as well as the character of God.

686 R. E. Murphy. "The Psalms: Prayer of Israel and the Church." *TBT* 32, no. 3 (1994): 133–37.

The Psalms have a universal appeal, to Israel and the church. The historical meaning is vital but we should remain open to a second, Christian, level of meaning.

6.6. Other

687 H. Birkeland. *The Evildoers in the Book of Psalms.* Oslo: Jacob Dybwad, 1955.

"The evildoers in the Book of Psalms are gentiles in all cases when a definite collective body or its representatives are meant. Israelite groups are included as far as cooperation with foreigners is concerned" (p. 93).

688 M. J. Buss. "The Psalms of Asaph and Korah." *JBL* 82 (1963): 382–92.

Titles attributing certain psalms to Asaph and Korah should not be dismissed in determining genre classifications. Psalms of Asaph and Korah collectively make up a general group of psalms that include the following genres: collective lament, Deuteronomic-levitical psalms of judgment, law and history, songs of Zion.

689 G. W. Anderson. "Enemies and Evildoers in the Book of Psalms." *Bulletin of the John Rylands University Library of Manchester* 48 (1965–66): 18–29.

The precise identification of the evildoers must be open to a variety of interpretations such as national enemies, personal illness, and slander. Summarizes major scholarly approaches to solving this question.

690 E. Slomovic. "Toward an Understanding of the Formation of Historical Titles in the Book of Psalms." *ZAW* 91 (1979): 350–80.

Psalm titles are not clues to fix the date of the psalms or their
headings, but examples of "connective midrash," that is, "a
midrash utilized by the rabbis in associating certain events or
personalities with various Psalms" (p. 352).

691 J. L. Mays. "The Place of Torah-Psalms in the Psalter." *JBL* 106
(1987): 3–12.
"The torah psalms point to a type of piety as setting-in-life for
the Psalms, a piety that used the entire book as prayer and
praise" (p. 12).

692 A. A. Anderson. "Psalms." Pp. 56–66 in *It Is Written: Scripture
Citing Scripture: Essays in Honour of Barnabas Lindars*. Edited
by D. A. Carson and H. G. M. Williamson. Cambridge: Cambridge University Press, 1988.
Discussion of the use of the OT in the Psalms (oracular
material, historical traditions, creation stories).

693 R. Chisholm Jr. "A Theology of the Psalms." Pp. 257–304 in *A
Biblical Theology of the Old Testament*. Edited by R. B. Zuck.
Chicago: Moody, 1991.
The theology of the Psalms is: God is universal Creator and
King who fights on behalf of his people. The proper response
is trust and praise.

694 D. Dhanaraj. *Theological Significance of the Motif of Enemies
in Selected Psalms of Individual Lament*. Orientalia Biblica et
Christiana, 4. Glückstadt: Augustin, 1992.
Discussion of nine lament psalms (3, 54, 5, 56, 59, 140, 143,
71). The enemies in these psalms are those who disparage the
psalmist's relationship to God. Includes critical translation of
these nine psalms.

695 S. Holm-Nielsen. "The Importance of Late Jewish Psalmody for
the Understanding of the Old Testament Psalmodic Tradition."
Studia theologica 14 (1960): 1–53.
Late (postexilic) Psalms have been typically denigrated in
scholarship because of a perceived stagnation in style (dependence on compositions). Rather, late psalmists' use of the OT
shows the importance that the canon played at the time.

696 G. T. Sheppard. "'Enemies' and the Politics of Prayer in the Book
of Psalms." Pp. 61–82 in *The Bible and the Politics of Exegesis*.
Edited by D. Jobling, P. L. Day, and G. T. Sheppard. Cleveland:
Pilgrim, 1991.

Applies socio-scientific (N. Gottwald) and canonical approaches to the Psalms to help interpret the imprecatory psalms.

697 R. J. Tournay. *Seeing and Hearing God with the Psalms: The Prophetic Liturgy of the Second Temple in Jerusalem.* Translated by J. E. Crowley. JSOTSup 118. Sheffield: JSOT, 1991.

Psalms have a prophetic dimension, that is, they transcend their own setting and are to be used as a means of hearing God's Word. This use of the Psalms can be seen in the liturgy of the Second Temple period.

698 W. S. Prinsloo. "A Comprehensive Semiostructural Exegetical Approach." *Old Testament Essays* 7, no. 4 (1994): 78–83.

Exegesis of the Psalter must pay more attention to the text rather than issues that have tended to dominate historical-critical research.

699 J. H. Eaton. *Psalms of the Way and the Kingdom: A Conference with the Commentators.* JSOTSup 199. Sheffield: Sheffield Academic, 1996.

Focuses on Psalms 1, 19, 119 (Torah) and 93, 97, 99 (kingship). In-depth "discussion" with ten nineteenth- and twentieth-century commentators.

7. Song of Songs

The Song of Songs (also known as the Song of Solomon and Canticles) is for some an odd, even scandalous, book to include in Holy Scripture. For others, it is a gem that speaks more directly to the heart than any other OT book. It remains a debated book, particularly in the areas of genre, unity, and proper interpretation.

7.1. Introductions

7.1.1. General

700 F. Godet. "Song of Songs." Pp. 241–331 in Godet's *Studies on the Old Testament*. London: Hodder & Stoughton, 1886.
> Broad, semipopular introduction which treats charter identifition divisions in the Song approaches to interpretation; origin.

701 W. E. Griffis. *The Lily among Thorns: A Study of the Biblical Drama Entitled The Song of Songs*. Boston/New York: Houghton Mifflin, 1890.
> Basic introductory issues, translation, and comments on a number of individual passages.

702 T. A. Goodwin. *Lovers Three Thousand Years Ago*. Chicago: Open Court, 1895.
> Popular introduction that aims to make the Song accessible to current readers. Includes discussion of the Song's historical import, its character, and an annotated translation.

703 P. Haupt. "The Book of Canticles." *American Journal of Semitic Languages and Literature* 18 (1902): 193–245; 19 (1903): 1–32.
   Translation with twelve extensive linguistic comments and numerous critical notes.

704 W. H. Schoff (ed.). *The Song of Songs: A Symposium.* Philadelphia: The Commercial Museum, 1924.
   Six essays on a broad range of topics: how the Song entered the canon; early and medieval Christian use; Greek and Hindu analogies; relation to fertility cult; political significance of the offering lists.

705 D. Broadribb. "Thoughts on the Song of Songs." *Abr-Nahrain* 3 (1961–62): 11–36.
   Reflections on various aspects of the Song that tend to be overlooked in commentaries: content, poetic structure, characters, scenes, development, relationship to OT, date, suggested emendations. The Song is a literary unity.

706 M. H. Segal. "The Song of Songs." *VT* 12 (1962): 470–90.
   Overview of various issues: stanzas, language and themes, authorship/date, composition/origin.

707 R. E. Murphy. "Form-Critical Studies in the Song of Songs." *Int* 27 (1973): 413–22.
   Structure, genre, life-setting, and intention of three of the songs. "The primary meaning of the Song would then have to do with human sexual love—the experience of it, its delights, its fidelity, and its power" (p. 422).

708 P. Kreeft. "Song of Songs: Life as Love." Pp. 97–141 in *Three Philosophies of Life.* San Francisco: Ignatius, 1989.
   Song of Songs is a love story, because God is love. It provides the answer to Qoheleth's question (what is life about?) and Job's quest (the need for God).

7.1.2. History of Scholarship

709 T. H. Gaster. "What 'The Song of Songs' Means." *Commentary* 13, no. 4 (1952): 316–22.
   Discusses general trends in the history of interpretation (ancient and modern).

710 R. E. Murphy. "Recent Literature on the Canticle of Canticles." *CBQ* 16 (1954): 1–11.

Review of several works from 1948 to 1953. Discussion of:
text and authorship; structure; parable or allegory; interpretation and canonization.

711 H. H. Rowley. "The Interpretation of the Song of Songs." Pp.
195–245 in *The Servant of the Lord and Other Essays in the Old
Testament*. Second Edition. Oxford: Blackwell, 1965.
History of interpretation (ancient and modern). No consensus yet exists as to its proper interpretation. See also Rowley's
"Song of Songs: An Examination of Recent Theory," *Journal
of the Royal Asiatic Society* (1938): 251–76.

712 R. E. Murphy. "Towards a Commentary on the Song of Songs."
CBQ 39 (1977): 482–96.
Brief overview of commentaries from 1960 to 1976. Discussion of various problems in the unity of the Song and its interpretation.

713 G. L. Carr. "Song of Songs." Pp. 281–95 in *A Complete Literary
Guide to the Bible*. Edited by L. Ryken and T. Longman III. Grand
Rapids: Zondervan, 1993.
Overview of the various interpretations of the Song throughout history. The Song is a poem rather than an anthology.

714 J. T. Dennison Jr. "What Should I Read on the Song of Solomon?"
Kerux 8, no. 2 (1993): 35–41.
Survey of recent approaches to the book. Includes review of
recent commentaries.

715 L. Zogbo. "Commentaries on the Song of Songs." *The Bible
Translator* 45 (1994): 343–48.
Review of several commentaries, particularly with respect to
linguistics and translation.

7.2. Origins and ANE Influence

Until the discovery of Mesopotamian parallels, the Song was often
thought to be simply an allegory of God's love for Israel, or, for Christians, Christ's love for the church. A comparison of the Song and various ANE counterparts, however, yields the inescapable conclusion
that the Song is "love poetry." Although this in and of itself does not
necessarily determine the proper interpretation of the Song, it does set
it within a particular literary context. The scholarly consensus, on the
basis of ANE parallels, is that the Song describes in explicit terms the
love between a man and a woman. For some, this love song may have

played some role in the Israelite cult, again working on the basis of ANE parallels, but this is far from conclusive.

716 T. J. Meek. "Canticles and the Tammuz Cult." *American Journal of Semitic Languages and Literature* 39 (1922–23): 1–14.

"There is scarcely an allusion in the whole of Canticles that does not call to mind some feature of the Tammuz cult and receive its simplest and easiest explanation from this source" (p. 9).

717 T. J. Meek. "Babylonian Parallels to the Song of Songs." *JBL* 43 (1924): 245–52.

Translation of a Babylonian text (*Keilschrifttexte aus Assur religiösen Inhalts*, vol. 4, no. 158) whose structure, themes, and phrases bear strong similarity to the Song of Songs.

718 S. Krauss. "The Archaeological Background of Some Passages in the Song of Songs." *JQR* 32 (1941–42): 115–37; 33 (1942–43): 17–27; 35 (1944–45): 59–78.

Discusses passages that describe the physical appearance of the bride and bridegroom.

719 A. Bentzen. "Remarks on the Canonisation of the Song of Songs." *Studia Orientalia* 1 (1953): 41–47.

Originally, the Song had a cultic function. Its connection with a special season of the year led to its inclusion in a musical collection. This led to canonization and subsequent attempts to rationalize its inclusion in the canon on religious grounds.

720 W. F. Albright. "Archaic Survivals in the Text of Canticles." Pp. 1–7 in *Hebrew and Semitic Studies Presented to Godfrey Rolles Driver in Celebration of His Seventieth Birthday, 20 August 1962*. Edited by D. W. Thomas and W. D. McHardy. Oxford: Clarendon, 1963.

There are no Greek loan-words in the Song, precluding a Hellenistic date. The Song of Songs was collected and edited in the fifth to fourth centuries B.C.

721 S. N. Kramer. "The Sacred Marriage and Solomon's Song of Songs." Pp. 85–106 in Kramer's *The Sacred Marriage Rite: Aspects of Faith, Myth, and Ritual in Ancient Sumer*. Bloomington: Indiana University Press, 1969.

Argues against Meek's thesis (#715) that the Song has its roots in the Canaanite Tammuz cult borrowed from Mesopotamia. Rather, the Sumerian Sacred Marriage songs provide closer parallels. See also "The Biblical 'Song of Songs' and the Sumerian Love Songs." *Expedition* 5 (1962): 25–31.

722 J. S. Cooper. "New Cuneiform Parallels to the Song of Songs." *JBL* 90 (1971): 157–62.

Comparison of the Sumerian "Message of Ludingira to His Mother" to the Song.

723 C. Rabin. "The Song of Songs and Tamil Poetry." *Studies in Religion* 3 (1973): 205–19.

Parallels to Tamil poetry suggest a First Temple date for the Song. See also #728.

724 J. B. White. *A Study of the Language of Love in the Song of Songs and Ancient Egyptian Poetry*. SBLDS, 38. Missoula: Scholars, 1978.

"The language of love in the Hebrew Song of Songs is reminiscent of the language used to describe love in the corpus of ancient Egyptian love poetry" (p. 17).

725 G. L. Carr. "Is the Song of Songs a 'Sacred Marriage' Drama?" *Journal of the Evangelical Theological Society* 22 (1979): 103–14.

Although the Song reflects many common ANE motifs and *topoi*, it is not a "sacred marriage drama" but lyric love poetry.

726 M. Sadgrove. "The Song of Songs as Wisdom Literature." Pp. 245–48 in *Studia Biblica 1978 I: Papers on Old Testament and Related Themes*. Edited by E. A. Livingstone. Sixth International Congress on Biblical Studies. JSOTSup 11. Sheffield: JSOT, 1979.

The Song is indisputably Yahwistic and may be regarded as wisdom literature: it is "an exploration into the riddle of human love, possibly in protest against polygamy" (p. 248).

727 M. V. Fox. "Love, Passion, and Perception in Israelite and Egyptian Love Poetry." *JBL* 102 (1983): 219–28.

Comparison of Egyptian love poetry and the Song will illuminate the character of each. "There is only one sexuality, one eros, and this pervades the universe projected by the lovers' imagery" (p. 228).

728 M. V. Fox. *The Song of Songs and Ancient Egyptian Love Songs*. Madison/Wisconsin/Lincoln: University of Wisconsin Press, 1985.

Exhaustive contribution that includes a translation with commentary and a far-ranging literary treatment covering such topics as function and social setting, major themes, and sources. Much of the Song is an artistic unity rather than a loose collection.

729 A. Mariaselvam. *The Song of Songs and Ancient Tamil Love Poems: Poetry and Symbolism*. Analecta Biblica, 118. Rome: Pontifical Biblical Institute, 1988.

Comparative study of the Song and Tamil love poems that also "aims at using the indigenous rhetoric and literary categories for classifying and appreciating the poems" in the Song (p. 22). See also #722.

730 D. J. A. Clines. "Why Is There a Song of Songs and What Does It Do to You if You Read It?" *Jian Dao* 1 (1994): 3–27.

Social, economic, and psychoanalytic investigation into the Song's origin. Effects of the Song on the history of interpretation and modern readers.

731 W. G. E. Watson. "Some Ancient Near Eastern Parallels to the Song of Songs." Pp. 253–71 in *Words Remembered, Texts Renewed: Essays in Honour of John F. A. Sawyer*. Edited by J. Davies et al. Sheffield: JSOT, 1995.

Comparison of Song of Songs and its ANE counterparts reveals "a common tradition within the love songs that have reached us through these texts, although each particular culture retained its own individual way of handling that tradition" (p. 266).

7.3. Structure and Unity

Is the Song a collection of independent songs or a unified literary composition? The discussion is certainly not at an end, whether or not the Song is a untitled work by a single author. Another issue that affects the question of unity is the Song's genre—whether it is drama, liturgy, song, or whether it has a plot.

732 N. H. Snaith. "The Song of Songs, The Dances of Virgins." *American Journal of Semitic Languages and Literature* 50 (1933–34): 129–42.

The Song is to be divided between alternating autumn and spring passages, corresponding to the agricultural year, the former associated with the youth-king seeking the maiden-princess; the latter, the maiden seeking the king.

733 S. B. Freehof. "The Song of Songs: A General Suggestion." *JQR* 39 (1948–49): 397–402.

What best explains the disorder of the material on the Song is that it is the description of a dream.

734 R. E. Murphy. "The Structure of the Canticle of Canticles." *CBQ* 11 (1949): 381–91.

There is no development or forward movement in the Song. It is simply a "series of scenes on an imaginative plane" (p. 383). There are six main divisions plus a conclusion.

735 F. Landesberger. "Poetic Units within the Song of Songs." *JBL* 73 (1955): 203–16.

The Song is not a unity but a collection of a large number of poems of varying length.

736 R. Kessler. *Some Poetical and Structural Features of the Song of Songs.* Leeds University Oriental Society Monograph Series, 8. 1965.

Study of those features (primarily repetition) that "reveal the craftsmanship behind the Song's poetry" (pp. 2–3).

737 J. C. Exum. " A Literary and Structural Analysis of the Song of Songs." *ZAW* 85 (1973): 47–79.

Isolates poetic units and examines their form and style, which demonstrate parallels among the poems. The Song is a work of unified authorship with an "intentional design" (p. 49).

738 W. E. Phipps. "The Plight of the Song of Songs." *JAAR* 42 (1974): 82–100.

The Song is an anthology of songs about intimate love, and hence should pose little difficulty in interpretation. Discusses trajectories in the history of Jewish and Christian interpretation.

739 R. E. Murphy. "The Unity of the Song of Songs." *VT* 29 (1979): 436–43.

Refrains, themes, and repetitions of words and phrases argue for unity.

740 W. H. Shea. "The Chiastic Structure of the Song of Songs." *ZAW* 92 (1980): 378–96.

The chiastic structure of the Song (A:B:C::C:B:A) demonstrates its unity.

741 M. Falk. *Love Lyrics from the Hebrew Bible: A Translation and Literary Study of the Song of Songs.* Bible and Literature Series, 4. Sheffield: Almond, 1982.

Rather than evincing a dramatic structure, "the Song has a variety of contexts which shift frequently in no apparent dramatic sequence and within which many different kinds of voices speak" (p. 3).

742 M. D. Goulder. *The Song of Fourteen Songs.* JSOTSup 36. Sheffield: JSOT, 1986.

The Song is "a semi-continuous sequence of fourteen scenes moving in a progression from the arrival of the Princess at Solomon's court to her acknowledgment by the King as his favorite queen" (p. 2).

743 M. T. Elliott. *The Literary Unity of the Canticle.* European University Series, 23—Theology 371. Bern: Peter Lang, 1989.

"A poetic analysis of the text of the Canticle disclose[s] eleven major elements of style which pervade the work, unify it, and argue strongly in favor of a single poet" (p. 260).

744 A. Brenner. "To See Is to Assume: Whose Love Is Celebrated in the Song of Songs?" *Biblical Interpretation* 1 (1993): 265–84.

The Song lacks plot and is therefore not a unity or an allegory.

7.4. Meaning

The explicit sexual imagery in the Song would naturally seem to invite debate as to its proper interpretation. The question of its proper interpretation is bound up to a large extent with the question of its original meaning (which is in turn dependent on its perceived connection to the ANE material) and its structure. If the Song was intended as a love poem, should that determine its interpretation in its canonical context? Why would such a love poem be included in the canon in the first place? Might it be that, although it fits comfortably in the genre of ANE love poetry, its ultimate meaning was intended to extend beyond those narrow boundaries? And how unified is the Song? If it is more than a collection of songs but a "story" with "plot," might that not further suggest that it is more than simply a celebration of human love? The variety of answers to these and other questions can be seen in the following sampling of works.

745 M. Friedländer. "The Plot of the Song of Songs." *JQR* 6 (1894): 648–55.

The shepherdess of the Song is not taken against her will to the king's palace in Jerusalem. The setting is pastoral.

746 J.-P. Audet. "The Meaning of the Canticle of Canticles." *Theology Digest* 5 (1957): 88–92. Original Title: "Le sens du Contique des Cantiques." *Revue Biblique* 62 (1955): 197–221.

Brief overview of the basic issues concerning interpretation. Conjugal love is a gift from God and reflects Genesis 2:24.

747 L. Cantwell. "The Allegory of the Canticle of Canticles." *Scripture* 16 (1964): 76–93.

Argues for the allegorical interpretation of the Song despite the "barrage of naturalist criticism" (p. 76) beginning in the nineteenth century. The Song is "an allegory of the new prophetical covenant" (p. 93).

748 P. Trible. "Love's Lyrics Redeemed." Pp. 144–65 in Trible's *God and the Rhetoric of Sexuality*. OBT. Philadelphia: Fortress, 1978. Reprinted in *A Feminist Companion to the Song of Songs*. Edited by A. Brenner. The Feminist Companion to the Bible, 1. Sheffield: JSOT, 1993, pp. 100–20.

The Song redeems the love that went awry in Genesis 2–3. "Genesis 2–3 depicted a tragedy of disobedience; the Song of Songs, a symphony of eroticism" (p. 162).

749 F. Landy. *Paradoxes of Paradise: Identity and Difference in the Song of Songs*. Bible and Literature Series 7. Sheffield: Almond, 1983.

The Song speaks to and for us today through a series of paradoxes culminating in the identification of the Song as a mirror-image of the Garden of Eden: "We leave what we love in order to live" (p. 275).

750 C. L. Meyers. "Gender Imagery in the Song of Songs." *HAR* 10 (1986): 209–23. Reprinted in *A Feminist Companion to the Song of Songs*. Edited by A. Brenner. The Feminist Companion to the Bible, 1. Sheffield: JSOT, 1993, pp. 197–212.

"Both the architectural and faunal images in the Song of Songs contain depictions of the female that are counter to stereotypical gender conceptions. These images convey might, strength, aggression, even danger" (p. 217).

751 R. M. Davidson. "Theology of Sexuality in the Song of Songs: Return to Eden." *Andrews University Seminary Studies* 27 (1989): 1–19.

Sexuality is part of God's creation. The Song celebrates the beauty of sexual love, but also calls for a typological interpretation; it "points beyond itself to the Lord of love" (p. 18).

752 A. Brenner (ed.). *A Feminist Companion to the Song of Songs.*
The Feminist Companion to the Bible, 1. Sheffield: JSOT, 1993.
Collection of twenty-one mostly previously published arti-
cles and essays on feminist interpretation of the Song of Songs.
Chapter headings include: Voices from the Past, Female
Authorship and Female Culture, Intertextual Connections
and the Critique of Patriarchy, Structure and Discourse, Genre
Interpretations.

753 M. Deckers. "The Structure of the Song of Songs and the Cen-
trality of *nepeš*." Pp. 172–96 in *A Feminist Companion to the
Song of Songs.* Edited by A. Brenner. The Feminist Companion
to the Bible, 1. Sheffield: JSOT, 1993.
The correct translation for *nepeš* is "being." The woman's
being is praiseworthy, for she intuitively understands that her
first obligation is to love the other person. Such feminine
imagery is symbolic of the people as a whole.

754 S. D. Goitein. "The Song of Songs: A Female Composition." Pp.
58–66 in *A Feminist Companion to the Song of Songs.* The Feminist Companion to the Bible, 1. Edited by A. Brenner. Sheffield:
JSOT, 1993.
The Song is both of folk origin and the product of a woman's
creative activity that linked the poems together motivated by
her own experiences.

755 R. N. Soulen. "The *waṣfs* of the Song of Songs and Hermeneutic." *JBL* 86 (1967): 183–90. Reprinted in *A Feminist Companion to the Song of Songs.* Edited by A. Brenner. The Feminist
Companion to the Bible, 1. Sheffield: JSOT, 1993, pp. 214–24.
The purpose of the detailed physical descriptions in the Song
(*waṣf* from the Arabic word meaning "description") is "a celebration of the joys of life and love at the same time an invi-
tation to share that joy" (p. 190).

756 J. W. Whedbee. "Paradox and Parody in the Song of Solomon:
Towards a Comic Reading of the most Sublime Song." Pp. 266–78
in *A Feminist Companion to the Song of Songs.* Edited by A.
Brenner. The Feminist Companion to the Bible, 1. Sheffield:
JSOT, 1993.
The use of parody and paradox by the author of the Song invites
a comic reading. Solomon is satirized "as an ostentatious king
whose image as a master of a great harem is undercut" (p. 276).

757 J. M. Munro. *Spikenard and Saffron: A Study of the Poetic Language of the Song of Songs.* JSOTSup 203. Sheffield: Sheffield Academic, 1995.

The complex of images in the Song of Songs functions not as "a philosophical treatise about love, but rather the experience of love, from the perspective of the woman" (p. 143).

758 E. R. Wendland. "Seeking the Path through a Forest of Symbols: A Figurative and Structural Survey of the Song of Songs." *Journal of Translation and Textlinguistics* 7 (1995): 13–59.

Application of a discourse-oriented, literary structural methodology. The theological message of the Song is that the love between a man and a woman is divinely established, "but which reaches beyond that to reflect upon the ineffable affection of the Lord for his people" (p. 13).

8. Lamentations

Although it would be too extreme to refer to Lamentations as a "neglected" OT book, the dearth of scholarly material, at least in English, certainly demonstrates that it has commanded surprisingly little attention when compared to most other books of the canon. The book consists of five poems (five chapters), the first four being acrostic (successive stanzas begin with the successive letter of the Hebrew alphabet, with each verse within that stanza beginning with that same letter). The book is appended, so to speak, in the English canon to Jeremiah (similarly in the LXX), but ascribing its authorship to Jeremiah has no explicit basis in the book itself. Hence, although an exilic date is highly likely, Lamentations is an anonymous work. Much of the scholarship on Lamentations has focused on its poetic composition, namely, its acrostic structure and the questions of meter and parallelism that are applied to other poetic books of the OT (see §5). Also, questions of ANE influence are raised, and the Mesopotamian world seems to provide a helpful context within which to view Lamentations. Its theological significance has been as fully explored as that of other books, but some have attempted to show how this sorrowful book reflects the exilic community's expression of their trust in God's justice in bringing this punishment against them. In view of the dearth of material, it seems best to organize the following works chronologically without further subdivision.

759 W. W. Canon. "The Authorship of Lamentations." *BSac* 81 (1924): 42–58.

Argues that Jeremiah authored Lamentations.

760 N. K. Gottwald. *Studies in the Book of Lamentations.* Studies in Biblical Theology, 37. Chicago: Alec R. Allenson, 1954. Reprinted: London: SCM, 1962.

"The aim of this monograph is to show in some detail that the Book of Lamentations has significance as the literary deposit of a critical historical era, that it possessed an important communal [liturgical] function and proclaimed a vital faith capable of adaptation to the storm and stress which attended the passing of the Hebraic Age" (p. 21). Discusses acrostic, genre, theology.

761 S. B. Gurewicz. "The Problems of Lamentations iii." *Australian Biblical Review* 8 (1960): 19–23.

All five chapters were not written during the same historical period. Chapter 3 may have been written by Jehoiachin during his imprisonment, before the destruction of Jerusalem.

762 T. F. McDaniel. "The Alleged Sumerian Influence upon Lamentations." *VT* 18 (1968): 198–209.

There is no "literary dependence or influence of the Sumerian lamentations on the biblical Lamentations" (p. 209). See #773 for the opposite view.

763 T. F. McDaniel. "Philological Studies in Lamentations I–II." *Bib* 49 (1968): 27–53, 198–209.

Ugaritic texts help clarify many lines in Lamentations. Also, Lamentations provides evidence for the pervasiveness of Northwest Semitic linguistic elements in ancient Hebrew.

764 B. Albrektson. *Studies in the Text and Theology of the Book of Lamentations: With A Critical Edition of the Peshitta Text.* Studia Theologica Lundensia, 21. Lund: Gleerup, 1963.

Text-critical observations on the Hebrew text in light of the LXX and Peshitta. Lamentations reflects a tension between faith and history. The Deuteronomic understanding of catastrophe as divine judgment helps relieve that tension.

765 S. T. Lachs. "The Date of Lamentations V." *JQR* 57 (1966): 46–56.

Argues for a Maccabean date for chapter 5 on the basis of parallels (language, events described, and mood) to 1 and 2 Maccabees and Josephus's *Antiquities of the Jews*.

766 J. L. Helberg. "The Incomparable Sorrow of Zion in the Book of Lamentations." Pp. 27–36 in *Studies in Wisdom Literature.* Edited by W. C. van Wyk. *Ou-Testamentiese Werkgemeenskap in Suid-Afrika,* 15–16. Potchesfstroom: Pro Rege, 1972–73.

Zion's suffering is incomparable because of her special personal relation to Yahweh. Yet her election to suffering allows her to trust Yahweh for deliverance. The poet's prayer brings this trust to the fore.

767 R. Gordis. "The Conclusion of the Book of Lamentations (5:22)." *JBL* 93 (1974): 289–93.

The final verse is crucial for understanding the whole. Reviews a number of interpretations and offers his own solution: the conjunction at the beginning of the verse, *kî 'im*, should be translated as "even if, although."

768 D. R. Hillers. "Observations on Syntax and Meter in Lamentations." Pp. 265–70 in *A Light unto My Path: Old Testament Studies in Honor of Jacob M. Myers*. Edited by H. M. Bream et al. Gettysburg Theological Studies, 4. Philadelphia: Temple University Press, 1974.

Analyzes the syntax of verbless clauses and postverbal elements in verbal clauses in the poetry of Lamentations and the prose of Pentateuch. The comparison of the two texts suggests that, although there are syntactical differences between them, the syntactical patterns in Lamentations are not to be explained on the basis of poetry's metrical demands.

769 W. F. Lanahan. "The Speaking Voice in the Book of Lamentations." *JBL* 93 (1974): 41–49.

The writer of Lamentations employs five personae worn by the poet through which he "perceives and gives expression to his world" (p. 41), to tell of Israel's grief.

770 M. J. Dahood. "New Readings in Lamentations." *Bib* 59 (1978): 174–97.

An examination of defective spellings in a number of passages, aided by the application of Northwest Semitic principles of grammar and prosody, helps clear up some misunderstandings in interpretation.

771 H. Gottlieb. *A Study on the Text of Lamentations*. Acta Jutlandica, 48; Theology Series, 12. Aarhus: Aarhus University Press, 1978.

Following Albrektson's text-critical observations (#763), Gottlieb adds his own where he takes issue.

772 W. H. Shea. "The *qinah* Structure of the Book of Lamentations." *Bib* 60 (1979): 103–7.

Lamentations as a whole evinces a *qinah* (a sorrowful poem written in 3:2 meter) structure, both on the small scale and the large scale, and hence should be taken as a unity. A broader discussion of *qinah* may be found in W. R. Garr, "The Qinah: A Study of Poetic Meter, Syntax and Style," *JBL* 95 (1983): 54–75.

773 W. C. Kaiser Jr. *A Biblical Approach to Personal Suffering.* Chicago: Moody, 1982.

Popular exposition of the relevance of Lamentations to personal suffering. Includes introductory chapter covering structure and background of Lamentations. The book portrays retributive suffering.

774 A. Mintz. "The Rhetoric of Lamentations and the Representation of Catastrophe." *Prooftexts* 2 (1982): 1–17.

Discusses the "national-collective nature of the Destruction, the trauma to the set of relations determined by the covenant, and the role of poetic language and its producers in the aftermath of the event" (p. 2).

775 W. C. Gwaltney. "The Biblical Book of Lamentations in the Context of the Near Eastern Lament Literature." Pp. 191–211 in *Scripture in Context II: More Essays on the Comparative Method.* Edited by W. Hallo et al. Winona Lake, Ind.: Eisenbrauns, 1983.

Analysis of the Mesopotamian lament genre. "There no longer exits a significant spatial and temporal gap between the Mesopotamian congregational form and the biblical book" (p. 194). See #761 for the opposite view.

776 M. S. Moore. "Human Suffering in Lamentations." *RB* 90 (1983): 534–55.

The author of Lamentations portrays his experience of suffering, which "becomes the focal-point for the grief work of an entire nation" (p. 554).

777 B. Johnson. "Form and Message in Lamentations." *ZAW* 97 (1985): 58–73.

Lamentations 3 is the center of the book. Chapters 1 and 2 describe the disaster, chapter 3 provides the theological answer (the disaster is God's punishment), which is further explained in chapters 4 and 5.

778 J. Renkema. "The Literary Structure of Lamentations I–IV." Pp. 294–396 in *The Structural Analysis of Biblical and Canaanite Poetry.* Edited by W. van der Meer and J. C. de Moor. JSOTSup 74. Sheffield: JSOT, 1988. See #547.

Exhaustive investigation yields an interconnected, concentric structure.

779 P. J. Owens. "Personification and Suffering in Lamentations 3." *Austin Seminary Bulletin: Faculty Edition* 105 (1990): 75–90.
   The suffering in Lamentations is not abstract but personified. The speakers of Lamentations 1–3 are personifications of "everyone's mother and father who may have been present at the catastrophe" (p. 86). The poet also personifies God as an anonymous enemy.

780 C. Westermann. *Lamentations: Issues and Interpretation*. Translated by C. Muenchow. Minneapolis: Fortress, 1991. Original Title: *Die Klagelieder: Forschungsgeschichte und Auslegung*. Neukirchener Verlag, 1990.
   Overview of twentieth century scholarship; basic issues in interpretation; exegesis; theological significance.

781 H. J. Bosman. "Two Proposals for a Structural Analysis of Lamentations 3 and 5." Pp. 77–98 in *Bible et Informatique*. Paris-Genève: Champion-Slatkine, 1992.
   Comparison of grammatical/syntactical analysis (computer database) and the more conventional literary approach (parallelism, word and theme repetition) of J. Renkema (#776). The two analyses are different and can be mutually supportive.

782 J. Krašovec. "The Source of Hope in the Book of Lamentations." *VT* 42 (1992): 223–33.
   Israel's sufferings are a function of her guilt, but God is merciful and his punishment is only for a limited time.

783 M. Saebo. "Who is 'The Man' in Lamentations 3? A Fresh Approach to the Interpretation of the Book of Lamentations." Pp. 294–306 in *Understanding Poets and Prophets: Essays in Honour of George Wishart Anderson*. JSOTSup 152. Edited by A. G. Auld. Sheffield: Sheffield Academic, 1993.
   The twin themes of Zion and the Davidic king may be the key to unlocking the meaning of the book. "The Man" in Lamentations 3 is the final Davidic king in Jerusalem, Zedekiah.

784 R. B. Salters. *Jonah and Lamentations*. Old Testament Guides. Sheffield: Sheffield Academic, 1994.
   Outline of the book; historical background; its poetry; authorship; genre; theology. Includes bibliography for each topic and of select commentaries.

Index of Modern Authors

Peter Enns is associate professor of Old Testament at Westminster Theological Seminary. He is the author of *Exodus Retold: Ancient Exegesis of the Departure from Egypt in Wis 10:15–21 and 19:1–9* (Harvard Semitic Monograph series) and *Exodus* in the NIV Application Commentary. His Ph.D. degree is from Harvard University.